The First English
DICTIONARY
of SLANG

1699

❦

Introduction by
JOHN SIMPSON

Bodleian Library
UNIVERSITY OF OXFORD

First published in 1699 by W. Hawes, P. Gilbourne, and W. Davis, London
as *A New Dictionary of the Terms Ancient and Modern of the Canting Crew,
In its several Tribes, of Gypsies, Beggers, Thieves, Cheats, &c.*, by B.E. Gent.

This edition first published in 2010 by

The Bodleian Library
Broad Street, Oxford OX1 3BG

www.bodleianbookshop.co.uk

ISBN 978 1 85124 348 8

Introduction © John Simpson, 2010
This edition © Bodleian Library, University of Oxford, 2010

Original title page, Douce E 106, © Bodleian Library,
University of Oxford, 2010

Cover design by Dot Little

Text designed and typeset in 11 on 13½ Monotype Van Dijck
by illuminati, Grosmont

Printed in the UK by CPI William Clowes, Beccles NR34 7TL
on Munken Premium Cream 80 gsm

A CIP record of this publication is available from
the British Library and the Library of Congress

A NEW
DICTIONARY
OF THE
Terms Ancient and Modern
OF THE
Canting Crew,
In its several
TRIBES,
OF
Gypsies, Beggers, Thieves, Cheats, &c.

WITH

An Addition of some Proverbs,
Phrases, Figurative Speeches, &c.

Useful for all sorts of People, (especially Foreigners) to secure their *Money* and preserve their *Lives*; besides very Diverting and Entertaining, being wholly New.

By *B. E.* Gent.

LONDON,
Printed for *W. Hawes* at the *Rose* in *Ludgate-street,* *P. Gilbourne* at the Corner of *Chancery-lane* in *Fleet-street,* and *W. Davis* at the *Black Bull* in *Cornhill.*

INTRODUCTION

A *New Dictionary of the Terms Ancient and Modern of the Canting Crew* (1699) by B.E. is a curiosity. It was a curiosity to its readers when it was first published, and in terms of the history of slang lexicography today it remains something of a curiosity to us too. But it is an important curiosity: it purported to deal with a subject that was of great interest to late-seventeenth-century readers, familiar with the perils of city life in post-Restoration London; the author's identity has always remained a mystery; the book itself offered an interpretation of urban life that is as black as it is lively.

It was the first dictionary to concern itself solely with slang vocabulary, or more specifically with 'cant'. Cant was the secret language of the rogues, beggars and vagabonds who peopled the underworld of early England. The word 'slang' itself is not recorded by the *Oxford English Dictionary* until 1756. The 'canting crews' mentioned in the title were the more or less organized groups of ne'er-do-wells who tricked and thieved their way through the country, by the seventeenth century often in small working units of two or three but doubtless much larger in the febrile popular imagination. Short lists of canting vocabulary had been available in print since at least the early sixteenth century, but they had always been tucked away in longer texts. B.E. was the first person to present the canting tongue in dictionary form.

Who was B.E.?

Almost nothing is known about the author of this dictionary. On the title page he describes himself as 'Gent.', implying that he regards himself as a man of some status in society. From the contents of his dictionary he appears to be well-read, familiar with current affairs and with some classical and modern languages. William J. Burke, in his *Literature of Slang* (1939), surmises that he was an antiquary,[1] defined by B.E. (in a manner comparable to Johnson's self-deprecating definition of a 'lexicographer') as 'a curious Critick in old Coins, Stones and Inscriptions, in Worm-eaten Records, and ancient Manuscripts; also one that affects and blindly doats, on Relicks, Ruins, old Customs, Phrases and Fashions'. Why B.E. chooses to include words like 'antiquary' in his dictionary is a question to which we shall return. On the basis of B.E.'s interests (to the extent that they are apparent from the contents of his dictionary) Julie Coleman builds a personality profile of him as someone who tends towards the Established Church and disapproves of religious or political factions, and in particular of dissenters who switch from one faction to another.[2] He shows a particular interest in naval matters and little respect for landlubbers. He may well have been a royalist and perhaps a Quaker. She tracks down two military officers, Brent Ely (or Eley) and Bernard Ellis, who might fit the bill, but admits that identification posited almost solely on field of interest and initials would be tenuous.

Why did B.E. choose to remain anonymous? Perhaps to chime in with the mystery of his subject matter, or perhaps to shield his identity from friends, or from the eyes of the law. Unlike the authors of other canting texts of the time he does not claim that he obtained his material through the dangerous expedient of consorting with rogues, but by his silence he does not exclude this possibility.

When was the dictionary published?

Here again we have a mystery. Over the last 150 years the dictionary has been variously dated between 1690 and 1720. There are two known impressions of the dictionary (more or less identical copies rather than two distinct editions). The impression most commonly found, and presumably that known to early researchers, had an undated title page. The celebrated Victorian slang lexicographer John Camden Hotten listed B.E.'s dictionary as published in 1710.[3] When an edition of B.E.'s dictionary was published in 1899, it was said on the spine to date from 1690. B.E. himself refers to the year 1695 in the text of the dictionary (at the entry for *Punchable*, 'old passable Money'),[4] a point which seems to have escaped some early scholars. Research into the period of activity of two of B.E.'s publishers (William Hawes and

Percivall Gilbourne) by William J. Burke in 1939 narrowed the date down to 1698,[5] but better bibliographical resources today move this window for all three publishers to 1699. The second, less well known impression of the dictionary is actually dated 1699 on the title page, and so this would seem to be the most likely date for a book perhaps first published undated in 1699 and rushed into a second printing (from the same plates) because of its unexpected popularity later that year. The major bibliographical sources today date both editions to 1699, and the dictionary was certainly being advertised in the *London Post* from May 1700, at the price of one shilling.

What sort of dictionary did B.E. claim to have written?

On his title page, B.E. described his dictionary as 'A New Dictionary of the Terms Ancient and Modern of the Canting Crew, In its several tribes, of *Gypsies, Beggers, Thieves, Cheats, &c.* With An Addition of some Proverbs, Phrases, Figurative Speeches, *&c.*' It had a twofold purpose: 'Useful for all sorts of People, (especially Foreigners) to secure their *Money* and preserve their *Lives*; besides very Diverting and Entertaining, being wholly New.'

Straightaway B.E. was tapping into the popular conception of the underworld, and bending it to his own advantage. His use of 'New' in the title is ambiguous: this type of dictionary was certainly new in English, but the title also suggests that it fits safely into a canting tradition. He will treat 'terms ancient and modern', as indeed he does, but

normally without making any distinction between old canting words and new ones. The picture of the present and the
past which he presents is cunningly merged into one. He
identifies the 'tribes' of canters: gypsies, beggars, thieves,
cheats, and others: but, as it turns out, his dictionary has
little or no link to the Roma (gypsies). And then, without
any introduction, he tells us that he is also adding other types
of lexical items which are not necessarily associated with
canting: proverbs, phrases, figurative speeches, and more.

This is not a dictionary in the modern style, with different types of words strictly classified and distinguished. It is
an amalgam of more or less related material based around
a canting theme, cleverly targeted at a general audience
which imagines (rightly or wrongly) that it needs advice
to 'secure' its money and 'preserve' its life, but which also
intends to 'entertain' and 'divert' through its claim to
expose a hidden way of life.

B.E.'s preface is undistinguished. He tells the reader the
then-familiar story of how Christianity brought the end of
slavery but the introduction of beggary. He dates English
beggary from the time of the dissolution of the monaster-
ies in Henry VIII's time, which was followed closely by
government legislation against beggars and vagabonds in
the reign of Queen Elizabeth I. In a passage which reads
xenophobically today, he claims that each country names
its gypsy class (like its sexual diseases) with reference
to countries which it regards as strange or inimical. His
comments indicate that he has little time for the Dutch
or the Swiss. Towards the end of his introduction he tries

to convince us that there is a connection between beggars and proverbs, before finally explaining his inclusion of some 'terms of better quality and fashion' with recourse to the argument that even the late-lamented Earl of Rochester (the famous debauchee John Wilmot) 'was not ashamed to keep the *Gypsies* Company'.

Fortunately the introduction is short, and does not prevent us from moving swiftly into the text of the dictionary itself. Indeed, it reads as something thrown off rapidly as publication day approached. Similarly B.E. does not provide the reader with any editorial apparatus, so the reader is left to his or her own devices to fathom the (albeit fairly simplistic) abbreviations and conventions of the dictionary.

But the slender preliminaries should not discourage the reader from embarking on the dictionary itself, which is in many ways a masterpiece. It is 'entertaining' enough for dipping into, but also short enough to make a sequential read enlightening. But before we examine the contents of the dictionary itself, it is necessary to know something about the underworld that B.E. sought to describe to his 'diverted' readers.

Gypsies and rogues of late medieval and early modern England

B.E.'s reference to 'gypsies' on his title page and in his introduction is misleading, and plays to popular misconceptions. From the late medieval period travellers and vagabonds had exercised the minds of legislators throughout Europe, as the various nations identified the problem of immigrant bands of gypsies and other travellers, and sought to move them on. English legislation directed against 'vagabonds' includes the Arrest of Night Walkers Act of 1331 (5 Edw. III, c. 14), which refers (in a mixture of Law French and Middle English) to 'diverses roberies, homicides, & felonies' committed by people called 'Roberdesmen, Wastours & Draghlacche' (see B.E.'s entries for *Roberds-men* and *Draw-Latches*). Similar warnings were made in the Vagabonds Act of 1383 (7 Rich. II, c. 1).

Vagabonds remained a problem, but the issue was compounded in the sixteenth century by 'gypsies', or 'Egyptians' as they were then known.[6] The Egyptians Act 1530 (22 Henry VIII, c. 10) sought to expel the 'outlandish people calling themselves Egyptians' (this act was not officially repealed until the mid-nineteenth century). Further legislation throughout the sixteenth century attempted to maintain and elaborate the official stance against 'Egyptians' and vagabonds.

Whatever the origin of these 'Egyptians', the legislation makes it clear that by the sixteenth century these were 'sham Egyptians' – or people adopting the pose of gypsies to pursue a vicarious life of roguery. They are said to have coloured their faces and to have hidden behind a guise of fortune-telling and begging as a front for various other illicit activities. Early Poor Law regulations put the onus on individual parishes to deal with the problem of wandering groups of vagabonds and Egyptians, and the parishes attempted to divide these into the deserving and undeserving poor – providing the minimum of support for those who 'deserved' benefit, and expelling the others. The movement of people in general out of the countryside and into the major towns and cities throughout this period led to the concentration of rogues and vagabonds in urban centres, and particularly in London. The population of London and other urban centres was from the mid-sixteenth century onwards additionally swelled by the influx of rootless soldiers and sailors returning from the European wars, many of whom mixed with the begging classes to eke out a threadbare existence. Immigration from Europe was another major factor of the population explosion which saw the citizenry of London increase eightfold between 1500 and 1650.[7] By the time of B.E.'s dictionary, London was a melting pot of the gentry, the middle classes, craftspeople and others: and the 'others' included many disaffected and 'masterless' drifters, as well as 'foreigners', who often spiralled unavoidably into a life of begging, crime and prostitution.

It must have been difficult for the more upright of the citizens of London and elsewhere to maintain a sense of perspective in relation to the underworld. How widespread was this threat? The public prints were full of lurid accounts of thieves, highwaymen, and others; public executions were commonplace, popular spectacles; the official penalties for what we might now regard as minor infringements of the law were harsh. And yet, as John McMullan has shown in his vivid account of 'The Canting Crew: London's Criminal Underworld 1550–1700', the relationship between the law and the begging and criminal underclasses was complex.

London at the time was divided into twenty-six 'wards', each with its own system of amateur policing. Constables, in London as elsewhere, were not employed as part of a regular, organized police force, but each ward was required to supply citizens to occupy this role on a temporary basis. The job was therefore regarded by many as irksome, and constables were subject to fines for wrongful arrest and other derelictions of duty. The system was clearly unsatisfactory, and led to a situation in which a dangerous relationship was engendered between enforcers of the law and potential wrongdoers. McMullan identifies the linchpin of this relationship as the 'fence', who acted as a go-between, clandestinely consorting with miscreants but at the same time negotiating the return of stolen property to its rightful owners.

Despite their irregular status, the constables were bound by strict regulations. The oath sworn by all constables included the following stern injunctions:

> You shall do your best endeavour (upon complaint to you made) to apprehend all Felons, Barretors, or Riotors, or persons riotously assembled, and persons making Affrays; and if any such Offenders shall make resistance with force, you shall levy Hue and Cry, and pursue them until they be taken. You shall do your best endeavour that the Watch in your Town be duly kept, and that Hue and Cry be duly pursued according to the Statutes; and that the Statute made for punishment of Rogues, Vagabonds, and Night-Walkers, and such other idle and wandring Persons coming within your Liberties be duly put in execution. You shall have a watchful Eye to such persons as shall maintain or keep any Common House or place, where

any unlawful Games or Plays are or shall be used; as also
to such persons as shall frequent or use such places, or
shall exercise or use any unlawful Games or Plays there,
or elsewhere, contrary to the Statute.[8]

The oath surveys many of the areas of activity which
perturbed the regular citizen in late-seventeenth-century
London, and covers many of the forms of crime or suspicious
behaviour that troubled the population of the capital city.

By the seventeenth century there were, moreover, areas
of London which were effectively no-go areas for the forces
of law. 'Sanctuaries' existed, in which church or civil
protection provided unofficial havens for the mixture of
the poor and the underworld that was attempting to keep
body and soul together below the radar of the legal estab-
lishment. The principal London 'sanctuaries', into which
constables and others entered at their peril, were located
in Southwark (Paris Garden, the liberties of the Clink and
the Mint), Newington, Whitefriars (Ram Alley), Spitalfields
and Whitechapel, and Newgate and Cripplegate.[9] These
areas were typically centres of poor housing stock set in
mazes of rat-run alleys, which functioned as the training
ground for rogues bound together in a loosely organized
confederacy of crime.

The literary representation of crime

The reality of crime in major urban centres was not the
only factor that affected the readership of B.E.'s dictionary.
The educated reader was also aware of a strand of literature
which depicted roguery. Both the reality and the literary

representation contributed to the air of mystery which surrounded his new dictionary of the canting crew.

Some of the first popular depictions of vagabonds and rogues can be found in the early and mid-sixteenth century. In 1528 Martin Luther produced an edition of the earlier *Liber Vagatorum*, detailing twenty-eight types or 'orders' of roving vagabonds in Germany, along with the deceits they practised on the unsuspecting.[10] The *Liber Vagatorum* included a vocabulary of beggars' cant (unrelated in content to the later English vocabularies). But this book was possibly known to the authors of the key English texts of the time: Robert Copland's *Hye Way to the Spittel House* (*c.* 1536), John Awdelay's *Fraternitie of Vagabondes* (1565), and Thomas Harman's *Caveat or Warening for Commen Cursetors* (1567). Harman was a Justice of the Peace who interrogated the poor who applied for parish relief. In his *Caveat* he listed various vagabonds by name as a means of bringing them to public notice. He also presented a short glossary of canting terms, again as a way of giving the enlightened citizen access to the world of the canters.

At this point the reality and the literary representation of the poor and the criminal might be taken as more or less coinciding. As time passed, the literary representation started to develop in its own direction. Robert Greene's cony-catching texts provided a more extensive view of the trickery and cheating of the thieving classes. In 1608 the dramatist Thomas Dekker published the first of a series of pamphlets depicting the life of the Bellman of London, one of the watchmen employed by the London wards to wander the streets by night complementing the daylight activities of the constables. Dekker offered his readers canting songs and also a list, based on Harman's, of the canting language, and this material was copied and elaborated by others who wished to expose and capitalize on the growing popular interest in the life of the underworld. These canting lists were still short, but Dekker noted, in his *Lanthorne and Candle-light* (1609) that 'it is impossible to imprint a Dictionarie of all the Canting phrases'.[11] That was an achievement that would apparently have to wait until the end of the century.

By the later seventeenth century this genre was showing no signs of letting up. Richard Head's *English Rogue* of 1665 borrows vocabulary lists from Harman and Dekker to build up a picture of the contemporary underworld. By now some of the canting vocabulary retailed by Head would have been obsolete on the streets, but was kept alive in the literary record. Head repeated his success in 1673 with his *Canting Academy*, again exposing villainy through description, songs and lists of the canting vocabulary. Further evidence of the popular interest in the underworld can be seen, as Julie Coleman has shown, in Restoration drama.[12] The relative freedom which the theatre enjoyed after the restrictions of Cromwell and the Commonwealth brought a libertine, picaresque style to the stage in which lovable rogues consorted with the gentry in fast-moving and contrived plots. Coleman has correctly identified some of the plays of Thomas Shadwell (especially *The Squire of Alsatia*, 1688 – in which 'Alsatia' is a canting name for the area of Whitefriars in London) as a link in the literary chain between Harman and B.E. By the late seventeenth century the underworld was a thriving literary theme, and one which B.E. was able to capitalize on in his explanatory dictionary.

B.E. and his canting dictionary

B.E.'s dictionary is only loosely about canting vocabulary. Overall his dictionary contains about 4,000 entries. Of these, only around 900 are marked (with a 'c.') as canting words and phrases. Some of these canting terms are perhaps two hundred years old, and did not form part of the canting vocabulary of his contemporaries.

The dictionary explores the themes of roguery and deceit: names for types of rogue (men and women), gulls or marks, fools, prostitutes, their tricks or cheats, untrustworthy servants, drinking, food, gaming, fighting and beating, money, officers of the law, places where crimes were committed, penalties and punishments, articles of jewellery and clothing, parts of the body, and the like. Throughout B.E.'s dictionary, the terminology and definitions are typically somewhat black and negative. Almost everything smacks of sham and deceit, and the artifice required to achieve this.

B.E. follows his predecessors in including the various 'orders' of the canting crew (the classification was intended to mirror the religious orders, especially mendicant friars). He lists two sets of orders within the dictionary: the five 'Old Orders', from 'Cursitors' to 'Sturdy-beggers', and twenty-seven 'New Ranks or Orders', from 'Rufflers' to 'Kinchin-morts'.[13]

Although B.E. bases his dictionary around canting terms, he chooses to fill out the text with other, related terms. These are typically words and phrases taken from everyday life, but which mirror the canting themes. He does not include words for law-abiding citizens (unless they happen to be gulls), but chooses words for or suggestive of fools, drunkards, rogues, soldiers, sailors, slatternly women, disease, street life, trade; in fact, anything that shows the negative side of life or that illustrates the sham, the odd, the eccentric, the outlandish, or extremes, contrast, and change. His chosen vocabulary is not that of the polite middle class, but of the alternative world, whether this is cant or other nonstandard terminology. And as we read the dictionary, we realize that B.E. senses that the mundane is not too far removed from the illicit.

Here is a typical sample of B.E.'s cant, for words beginning with *fa* (he maintains alphabetical order in general, varying this slightly when it suits his purpose):

Facer, c. a Bumper without Lip-room.
Fag, c. to Beat.
Fag'd, c. Beaten.
Fag the Bloss, c. bang the Wench.
Fag the Fen, c. drub the Whore.
Faggot the Culls, c. Bind the Men.
Famms, c. Hands.
Fambles, c. Hands.
Famble-cheats, c. Gold-rings, or Gloves.
Famgrasp, c. to agree or make up a Difference. *Famgrasp the Cove*, c. to agree with the Adversary.
Farting-crackers, c. Breeches.

Fastner, c. a Warrant.
Fat Cull, c. a rich Fellow.
Faulkner, c. see Tumbler, first Part.
Faytors, c. the Second (old) Rank of the Canting Crew.

Of these words, several derive from the canting lists to which B.E. had recourse. *Fambles*, for example, is an old term, and dates back to Harman and Dekker, and was copied by Head; *famble-cheats* echoes Harman's *fambling-chete* (also in Dekker), while Head prefers B.E.'s form; *famgrasp the cove* crops up in Head; *faytors* appears in Dekker. It is possible that B.E. took some of his material from Randle Holme's *Academy of Armory* (1688), which, despite its title, contained lists of thieves' cant, plumbers' terms, linguistic vocabulary, and much more alongside its traditional armorial content. But not all of B.E.'s terms have been found in earlier texts; he seems to have drawn to a certain extent on his own experience and reading to assemble additional material. Furthermore, he worked closely with Elisha Coles's *English Dictionary* of 1676. Coles's dictionary was the first monolingual dictionary of English to include a broad range of general terms, and it also included a scattering of canting terms (labelled with a 'c.', a device which B.E. adopted). B.E. was indebted to Coles for many suggestions and turns of phrase.[14]

The fourteen cant terms listed above are interspersed with around forty other words and phrases in the section beginning with *fa*. Within this range we find the following non-canting terms:

Face in Wine, the Colour.

Factitious, Bodies made by Art, as Glass, Paper, and all Compound or made Metals, as Brass, Steel, Pewter, Latin, *&c.*

Fadge, it won't fadge or doe.

Fallacies, Cheats, Tricks, Deceipts.

Falter, to fail or more particularly a failure, or Trip of the Tongue, entangled with the Palsy, produced also from excess of Drink, or Guilt.

Family of Love, Lewd Women, Whores; also a Sect.

Fantastick, Whimsical, Freakish, or Capricious. *A Fantastick Dress*, very particular, remarkable.

Fastnesses, Boggs.

Fat, the last landed, inned or stow'd of any sort of Merchandize whatever, so called by the several Gangs of Water-side-Porters, *&c.*

B.E. delights in showing that day-to-day vocabulary ('*Falter*, to fail') is only one step away from the themes of canting ('more particularly a failure, or Trip of the Tongue, entangled with the Palsy, produced also from excess of Drink, or Guilt'), in this case disease, drink, and punishment. He is pleased to report that '*Family of Love*' describes 'Lewd Women, Whores', but also means 'a Sect', which, according to the *Oxford English Dictionary*, 'held that religion consisted chiefly in the exercise of love, and that absolute obedience was due to all established governments, however tyrannical'. The dictionary is full of counterpoints such as this.

B.E.'s coverage of the language is patchy. But when he finds a word which fits one of his thematic categories, he plays it for all it is worth. Take, for instance, his full entry for '*face*' (with my comments in brackets):

Face in Wine [drink], the Colour. *A good Face*, a very fine bright Colour [extreme/contrast]. *To make a Face*, to make a show or feign [dissembling]; also to wryth contract or distort the Face in Contempt or Derision [distortion/derision]. *To set a good Face upon a bad Cause, or Matter*, to make the best of it [contrast of good and bad]. *A good Face needs no Band*, or no advantage to set it off [lack of artifice]. *The Broad-fac'd Bird, or the Bird that is all Face under Feathers*, a Periphrasis for an Owl [extreme/contrast]. *Face about to the Right or Left*, turn about [contrast]. *to Face Danger*, to meet it [danger]. *Facing of the Sleeve*, the Turn-up [contrast].

So B.E.'s themes derive from his core canting vocabulary, but attract similar nonstandard vocabulary from everyday life. Even his phrases and proverbs typically illustrate contrast ('*Over-shoes over Boots*, or to go Through-stitch', '*The Pitcher do's not go so often to the Well, but it comes home Broke at last*, of him that after many lucky Adventures or narrow Escapes, miscarries in the End', '*No Smoke but there is some Fire*', etc.).

Some further examples of contrast, sham, and artifice:

Mutton-in-long-coats, Women. *A Leg of Mutton in a Silk-Stocking*, a Woman's Leg.

Muzzle, c. a Beard, (usually) long and nasty.

Nice, squeemish, precise. *More nice than wise, a Sir Courtly Nice*, a silly empty, gay, foolish Fellow.

Night-rale, a Woman's combing Cloth, to dress her Head in.

Nooz'd, or *caught in a Nooze*, married; also Hanged.

Old Harry, a Composition used by Vintners, when they bedevil their Wines.

> *Orator to a Mountebank*, the Doctor's Decoy who in conjunction with Jack Pudding, amuses, diverts and draws in the Patients.
>
> *Over-sight*, has two contrary Significations under one Sound, for an Oversight is either the Care or Charge of, or Inspection into any Affair, or else an Oversight Imports a Slip or Error committed in it, for want of due Care and Circumspection.

Another of B.E.'s practices is to include a term because of its similarity to another adjacent term, perhaps to help the reader to disambiguate the words, or to point out a similarity or contrast. He selects *factitious*, presumably as a word recalling artifice, and pairs it with the (then) positive *facetious*:

> *Facetious*, full of Merry Tales and Jests, pleasantly merry.
>
> *Factitious*, Bodies made by Art, as Glass, Paper, and all Compound or made Metals, as Brass, Steel, Pewter, Latin, *&c.*

After selecting one *faggot* word from cant, he slides in a non-canting soldiering word:

> *Faggot the Culls*, c. Bind the Men.
>
> *Faggots*, Men Muster'd for Souldiers, not yet Listed.

The canting *fastner*, from the theme of justice, allows B.E. to elaborate on other *fast* words, one of which is positive, with the other denoting something unstable (perhaps suggested by Coles's entry). B.E. seems to enjoy the uncomfortable affinities.

> *Fast-friends*, sure or trusty.

Fastner, c. a Warrant.
Fastnesses, Boggs.

By contrast, B.E. also decides to include a subset of higher-status words, often from hunting or country life in general. From John Guillim's early-seventeenth-century *Display of Heraldrie* he plucks names for wildlife (foxes, deer, hares, etc.).[15] He also borrows from lists of the sounds these animals make, or of the specific names given to them at different periods of their life cycle. The terms of hawking, too, make an appearance. He includes terms for religious groups (Latitudinarians, Unitarians, etc.), which he seems to regard with as much disdain as he does anyone else who dissents from the middle way.

The two longest entries in the dictionary explore the canting terms *queer* and *rum. Queer* ('base, Roguish, naught') is followed by over twenty related expressions, illustrating B.E.'s customary themes:

Queere-cuffin, c. a Justice of Peace; also a Churl.
Queere-cull, c. a Fop, or Fool, a Codshead; also a shabby poor Fellow.
Queere-degen, c. an Iron, Steel, or Brass-hilted Sword.
Queere-diver, c. a bungling Pick-pocket.
Queere-doxy, c. a jilting Jade, a sorry shabby Wench.
Queere-drawers, c. Yarn, coarse Worsted, ord'nary or old Stockings.
Queere-duke, c. a poor decayed Gentleman; also a lean, thin, half Starved Fellow.

Rum was used in canting language at the time in a positive sense ('good, fine').

Rum-booze, c. Wine; also very good or strong Drink.
Rum-boozing-Welts, c. bunches of Grapes.
Rum-beck, c. any Justice of the Peace.
Rum-bob, c. a young Prentice; also a sharp, sly Trick, and a pretty short Wig.
Rum-bite, c. a cleaver Cheat, a neat Trick.
Rum-bleating-cheat, c. a very fat Weather.
Rum-blower, c. a very Handsom Mistress, kept by a particular Man.

By a quirk of language, our modern words *queer* and *rum* (both meaning 'odd, strange') are etymologically distinct from B.E.'s terms: he would have been amused by the interplay between the four words.

A continuous sequence of non-canting terms illustrates how B.E.'s selection of material reflects the themes he found in the language of the canters, and his delight in discovering similar themes throughout the nonstandard vocabulary of late-seventeenth-century England:

Carouse, to Drink hard, or Quaff heartily.
Carpet-road, Level and very good.
Carriers, Pigeons that will with safety, and almost incredible Swiftness convey Letters from one Place to another, much used at *Smyrna* and *Aleppo*; also Milk-womens Hirelings, or Servants, that carry the Pail Morning and Evening.
Carrots, Red hair'd People, from the Colour of the well known Root of that Name, whence came
Carrot-pated, used in derision.
Carted-Whore, Whipt publickly, and packt out of Town. *The Cart before the Horse*, of a thing preposterous, and out of Place.

Conclusion

Like Randle Holme's *Academy of Armory*, B.E.'s dictionary is not what it claims on the title page. He starts with a core of canting terms, often taken from earlier texts but redolent of what his readers would have regarded as the 'Hellish Linguists'[16] or canters of the day. Having established the themes of thievery, prostitution, gaming, drinking, and general deceit and sham (even a wig or a periwig symbolizes artifice), he expands the content of his dictionary to include comparable or parallel terms especially from everyday non-standard vocabulary. His selection of entries is influenced by his experience of the world, and by his playful interest in the contrasting senses of individual words, and the semantic difference between similar-sounding words. His attitude to language leaves the reader with the uncomfortable feeling that urban life in the late seventeenth century was a precarious existence, surrounded by danger and artifice, but fascinating and diverting when viewed from the perspective of the vagaries of the language.

B.E.'s dictionary was the first slang dictionary in English, but in some ways it was a side alley in the development of lexicography. It was influential, but perhaps not in the way B.E. would have liked. In 1725 another canting dictionary was published, entitled *A new canting dictionary: comprehending all the terms, ancient and modern, used in the several tribes of gypsies, beggars, shoplifters, highwaymen, foot-pads, and all other clans of cheats and villains. Interspersed with proverbs, phrases, figurative speeches, &c.* The title is in homage to (or at least imitation of) B.E., but the dictionary itself is divested of B.E.'s non-canting content. Later canting literature builds more on the 1725 publication than on B.E.'s original dictionary. We have to wait until the end of the eighteenth century and the early years of the nineteenth century for more comprehensive dictionaries that pick up the theme of general slang that B.E. initiated.

Notes

1. William Jeremiah Burke, *The Literature of Slang* (New York: New York Public Library, 1939), p. 65/2.

2. Julie Coleman, *A History of Cant and Slang Dictionaries*, Volume 1: *1567–1784* (Oxford: Oxford University Press: 2004), pp. 99–101.

3. John Camden Hotten, 'Bibliography of Slang, Cant, and Vulgar Language', in *Dictionary of Modern Slang, Cant, and Vulgar Words* (London: J.C. Hotten, 1859), pp. 147–60.

4. 'Act 7 & 8 William & Mary, c. 1 §9 (1695–6) stipulated that hammered coins in circulation and not damaged by clipping should be "struck through ... with a solid Punch" before being circulated further, as a means of preventing clipping' (*OED*). The term was obsolescent in B.E.'s day.

5. Burke, *The Literature of Slang*, p. 65/2.

6. See, for example, David Mayall, *Gypsy Identities, 1500–2000: From Egipcyans and Moon-men to the Ethnic Romany* (London: Routledge, 2001), and Janet Sorensen 'Vulgar Tongues: Canting Dictionaries and the Language of the People in Eighteenth-Century Britain', in *Eighteenth Century Studies*, vol. 37, no. 3 (2004), pp. 435–54.

7. John L. McMullan, *The Canting Crew: London's Criminal Underworld 1550–1700* (New Brunswick NJ: Rutgers University Press, 1984), p. 8.

8. Robert Gardiner, *The Compleat Constable* (1692), pp. 10–11.

9. McMullan, *The Canting Crew*, pp. 55–63.

10. John Camden Hotten, ed., *The Book of Vagabonds and Beggars: With a Vocabulary of their Language. Edited by Martin Luther in the Year 1528. Now first translated into English, with Introduction and Notes* (London: J.C. Hotten, 1860). According to Hotten 'The *Liber Vagatorum*, or

The Book of Vagabonds, was probably written shortly after 1509'
(p. xv).

11. Thomas Dekker, *Lanthorne and Candle-light; Or, The Bell-mans Second Nights-walke* (1609), sig. C1.

12. Coleman, *A History of Cant and Slang Dictionaries*, p. 91.

13. B.E. inadvertently lists both the 'Swadlers' and the 'Whip-Jacks' as belonging to the tenth order; his sources place the 'Whip-Jacks' in the nineteenth order. 'Whip-Jacks' are 'Counterfeit Mariners Begging with false Passes, pretending Shipwrecks, great Losses at Sea, &c. narrow escapes; telling dismal Stories, having learnt *Tar-terms* on purpose, but are meer Cheats.'

14. For a fuller analysis of the contents and structure of B.E.'s dictionary see Coleman, *A History of Cant and Slang Dictionaries*, pp. 76–104 and Appendix A; and Maurizio Gotti's excellent chapter on 'B.E.'s Innovative Approach', in *The Language of Thieves and Vagabonds: 17th and 18th Century Canting Lexicography in England* (Tübingen: Niemeyer, Lexicographica Series Maior 94, 1999), pp. 60–67.

15. Coleman, *A History of Cant and Slang Dictionaries*, p. 89.

16. *The Confession and Execution as well of the several Prisoners that suffered at Tyburn on Wednesday the 17th of April 1678* (London, 1678), p. 5: '*George Dogget* was Executed upon his Condemnation the last Sessions before this. His Crime was picking a Watch out of a Gentlemans pocket, and that even at Church. He had long and notoriously been concern'd in Fending [i.e. Fencing], that is, as those Hellish Linguists understand the Canting word, receiving and putting off stolen Goods.'

THE PREFACE

BEFORE I present the Reader, with the following
Dictionary of the Beggers and Gypsies Cant, I think
it not amiss to premise a few Words concerning the Beggers
and Gypsies themselves, by way of an Historical Account,
of the Antiquity of the one, and the Universality of the
other.

It makes not a little for the Honour of the Beggers,
that their Original according to some Accounts, is no less
Ancient than that of Christianity it self; for in the Opinion
of Charron, as the Slaves went off, the Beggers came in
their Place. So much at least is granted, That the Jews
who allow'd of Slaves, had no Beggers. What shall we say,
but that if it be true, that the Emancipating or Freeing
of Slaves was indeed the making of Beggers; it follows
that Christianity which is daily employed in Redeeming
Slaves from the Turks, Ransom'd no less than all at once
from Pagan Slavery at first, at no dearer a Rate, than the
Rent-charge of maintaining the Beggers, as the Price and
Purchase of our Freedoms.

As for the Antiquity of the English Beggers, it may be observed, That the first Statute which makes Provision for the Parish-Poor, is no older than Queen Elizabeth; from which it may be fairly Collected, That they entred with us upon the Dissolution of the Abbeys, as with them abroad, upon the Delivery of the Slaves.

For the Gypsies, they and the Foul Disease have alike the Fate to run through a Geography of Names, and to be made free of as many Countries, as almost there are Languages to call them Names in; for as the French call the Pox the *Italian* Disease, they again give it to the Spaniards, as these to the French; so the French call the Gypsies *Boemie*, or *Bohemians*, belike, because they made their first Appearance in Bohemia of any Part of Europe; the Italians Name them *Zingari* or *Saracens*, the Spaniards *Itanos* as we *Egyptians*; whether it be, that the Italians give them the Turks, as the Spaniards give them the Moors, as being both the next Neighbors to each; I take not upon me to Determine, only it may be observed, betwixt the Complement of either kind, the Odds is no greater than this, of giving a Nation a Clap, or of laying a brood of Bastards at it's Door.

Though Holland has no Beggers, if the Dutch themselves are not the greatest Beggers in the World; and Switzerland has no Thieves, if the Swiss who are altogether Soldiers, are not the greatest of Thieves. Yet, I say, neither the States that are without Beggers, nor the Cantons that are without Thieves, are notwithstanding either the one or the other, without Gypsies. So as what they want of Beggers and Thieves in point of Antiquity, the Gypsies claim above both, in point of Universality.

But though Gypsies are found in all Christian Countries, yet are they not in all Countries alike; their Nature and Genius being diverse, in proportion to the Countries amongst whom they Stroul; so that the same Question remains upon them, as is started of the Winds, as Universal Travellers as the Gypsies, that it seems a Doubt, Whether they partake more of the Nature of the Countries whence they rise, or of those through which they Pass?

Nor is it also new to meet the Beggers and the Proverbs together, for the Fashion is as old as Plautus, who puts the Proverbs and the Jests in the Mouth of his Slaves. And in the Character of Sancho Pancha, Cervantes has Trod in the same Steps; in the History of Don Quixot, Sancho being distinguished no less by his Proverbs, than his Asse. And between the Slaves and the Beggers, the Difference is no greater, than between Fathers and their Heirs.

If some Terms and Phrases of better Quality and Fashion, keep so ill Company, as Tag-Rag and Long-Tail; you are to remember, that it is no less then Customary, for Great Persons a broad to hide themselves often in Disguises among the Gypsies; and even the late L. of Rochester among us, when time was, among other Frolicks, was not ashamed to keep the Gypsies Company.

A NEW DICTIONARY

A

Abram-cove, c. a Naked or poor Man, also a lusty strong Rogue.

Abram-men, c. the seventeenth Order of the Canting-crew. Beggers antickly trick'd up with Ribbands, Red Tape, Foxtails, Rags, *&c.* pretending Madness to palliate their Thefts of Poultrey, Linnen, *&c.*

Academy, c. a Bawdy-house, also an University, or School to learn Genteleman like Exercises.

Acoutrements, c. fine rigging (now) for Men or Women, (formerly) only Trappings for Horses. *Well accoutred*, c. gentilly dress'd.

Acquests, and *Acquisitions*, the rights of Fortune purchased by Labour, Arts or Arms, oppos'd to Hereditary and Paternal.

Acteon, a Cuckold.

Acteon'd, Cuckolded, or made a Cuckold of.

Adam's-ale, Water.

Adam-tiler, c. a Pickpocket's Camerade, who receives Stolen Money or Goods, and scowers off with them.

Addle-pate, one full of Whimsies and Projects, and as empty
   of Wit.

Addle-plot, a Martin-mar-all.

Adrift, loose. *I'll turn ye adrift*, a Tar-phrase; I'll prevent ye
   doing me any harm.

Affidavit-men, Knights of the Post, Mercenary Swearers for
   Hire, Inhabitants (formerly) of White Friers, now
   dispersed.

Aft and *Abaft*, towards the Stern, or hinder Part of the Ship.

Aim, Endeavour or Design. *To aim*, or *level at a Mark*, *he has
   mist his Aim or End.*

Air of a Song, the Tune.

Air of a Face or Picture, the Configuration and consent of
   Parts in each.

Airy, Light, brisk, pleasant; also a Nest of Hawks. He is an
   Airy Fellow.

Alabaster, mixt by all the knavish Perfumers with the Hair-
   Powder they sell, to make it weigh heavy, being of it
   self very cheap, that their Gain may be the greater,
   found destructive to the Hair and Health.

Alsatia, White Friers.

Alsatia the higher, the same.

Alsatia the lower, the Mint in Southwark.

Alsatians, the Inhabitants, such as, broken Gentlemen,
   Tradesmen, &c. Lurking there.

Allay, the Embasing of a purer and finer Metal, by mixing
   it with an inferior or coarser Metal, as of pale Gold
   with a Silver-Allay, or of deep Gold with an Allay of
   Copper; also whatever is used to qualify what is bitter
   or nauseous in Compositions, as gilding of Pills,
   sweetning of Boluses, or Powders.

Aloft, above or over Head; also anciently an Upper-room or Garret, now more us'd in Compounds, as *Cock-loft*, *Hay-loft*, *&c.*

Altemall, altogether.

Altitudes, the Man is in his Altitudes, he is Drunk.

Ambidexter, one that goes snacks in gaming with both Parties; also a *Lawyer* that takes Fees of *Plaintif* and *Defendant* at once.

Ambient-Air, Air a-broad oppos'd to that pent and shut up in Wells, Vaults, Caves, *&c.* Or else the outward Air in the House, oppos'd to that shut up in the Cavities of Vessels, Glasses, Vials, *&c.*

Ambrol, among the Tarrs for Admiral.

Amphibious Creatures of a doubtful kind, or of a double Element; as a Bat is between a Bird and a Beast; an Otter between a Beast and a Fish; and a Puffin with the rest of the Sea-Fowl, between Fowl and Fish.

Amuse, to throw dust in one's Eyes, by diverting one from a serious Thought to a pleasant one.

Amusement, a Blind or Disengagement from deep Thoughts to more Diverting.

An Ark, c. a Boat or Wherry.

Anglers, c. Cheats, petty Thievs, who have a Stick with a hook at the end, with which they pluck things out of Windows, Grates, *&c.* also those that draw in People to be cheated.

Animal, a Fool. *He is a meer Animal*, he is a very silly Fellow.

Antechambers, forerooms for receiving of Visits, as the back and Drawing Rooms are for Lodgings, anciently called Dining-rooms.

Antidote, a very homely Woman, also a medicine against Poyson.

Antient, at Sea, for Ensign, or Flag.

Anticks, little Images on stone, on the out side of old Churches. *Antick postures or dresses*, such as are odd, ridiculous and singular, the habits and motions of Fools, Zanies, or Merry-andrews, of Mountebanks, with Ribbands, mismatched colours and Feathers.

Antiquary, a curious Critick in old Coins, Stones and Inscriptions, in Worm-eaten Records, and ancient Manuscripts; also one that affects and blindly doats, on Relicks, Ruins, old Customs, Phrases and Fashions.

Antiquated-Rogue, Old, out of date, that has forgot or left off his Trade of Thieving, *&c.* also superannuated, obsolete Customs, or Words, such as are worn out, out of use and Fashion.

Apart, severally, asunder.

Apartments, Rooms apart, private Lodgings, inner Chambers, secret and withdrawn from the rest. Recesses of the House opposed to the *Ante-chambers*.

Arack, an East-Indian Brandy, or strong Spirit drawn from Rice, and (sometimes) Roes of Fish, best when old, much us'd in Punch, the double distill'd *Goa* most esteem'd.

Arch, { *Rogue*, Witty. / *Wag*, Pleasant. / *Whore*, Cunning.

Arms, to bear Arms, a Profession not unbecoming a Gentleman, for *Books* and *Arms* are Gentlemens Burdens.

Armour, in his Armour, Pot-valiant.

Aristippus, a Diet-drink, or Decoction of *Sarsa, China, &c.*
Sold at certain Coffee-houses, and drank as *Tea.*

Arsworm, a little diminutive Fellow.

Ascendant, Power, Influence, as *he has the Ascendant over him*,
or an Hank upon him; also the Horoscope, or point of
the Ecliptic that rises at one's Nativity.

Assig, now us'd for Assignation, an Appointment or
Meeting.

Assuming, conceited, as, *an Assuming Fellow*, one that
abounds in his own Sense, and imposes it upon every
Man else.

Assurance, Confidence, as, *a Man of Assurance*, one that has a
stock of Confidence.

Aunt, A Bawd, as *one of my Aunts*, one of the same Order.

Autem, c. a Church, also Married.

Autem mort, c. a Married-woman, also the Twenty fourth
Order of the Canting Tribe, Travelling, Begging (and
often Stealing) about the Country, with one Child in
Arms, another on Back, and (sometimes) leading a third
in the Hand.

Auxiliary beauty, Dress, Paint, Patches, setting of Eye-
brows, and licking the Lipps with red.

B

Babler, a great Talker.

Backt, Dead, as *he wishes the old Man backt*, he longs to have his Father upon six Mens shoulders, or as *his Back's up*, he is in a fume or angry.

Bacon, as *he savd his Bacon*, he has escap'd with a whole Skin. *A good voice to beg Bacon*, said in jear of an ill voice.

Badge, a mark of Distinction among poor People; as, Porters, Water-men, Parish-Pensioners and Hospital-boys, Blew-coats and Badges being the ancient Liveries.

Badgers, they that buy up a quantity of Corn and hoard it up in the same Market, till the price rises; or carry it to another, where it bears a better. Also a Beast for sport, *Badger Eartheth*, *Lodgeth*.

Badjob, an ill bout, bargain, or business.

Baffle, to worst, or defeat. *A baffled Cause*, worsted, defeated.

Baggage, a Whore or Slut.

Bagonet or *Bionet*, a *Dagger*.

Bail-dock, the place in the Court, where the Prisoners are kept till called to be Arraign'd.

Balsom, c. Money.

Balderdash, ill, unpleasant, unwholesom mixures of Wine, Ale, *&c.*

Banbury-story, of a Cock and a Bull, silly chat.

Banditti, Highway-men, (Horse or Foot) Rogues of any kind, now, but strictly Italian Outlaws.

Bandog, a Bailiff, or his Follower, a Sergeant, or his Yeoman; also a very fierce Mastive.

Bandore, a Widows mourning Peak; also a Musical Instrument.

Bandy, a play at Ball with a Bat; also to follow a Faction.

Bandy-legg'd, crooked.

Bang, a blow, *to Bang*, to beat.

Banillas, a Seed growing in a Cod, somewhat resembling a Kidney-bean, on Trees in the *Indies*, much us'd in Chocolate.

Banter, a pleasant way of prating, which seems in earnest, but is in jest, a sort of ridicule, *What do you banter me?* i.e. do you pretend to impose upon me, or to expose me to the Company, and I not know your meaning.

Bantling, a Child.

Barker, a Salesman's Servant that walks before the Shop, and cries, Cloaks, Coats, or Gowns, what d'ye lack, Sir?

Barketh, the Noise a Fox makes at Rutting time.

Barnacle, c. a good job, or a snack easily got, also Fish growing on Ships sides when foul, and a Brake for unruly Horses Noses, also the Gratuity to *Jockeys*, for selling or buying Horses.

Barnadcles, c. the Irons Fellons wear in Goal.

Bar-wig, between a bob and a long one.

Basset, a Game at Cards.

Baste, to beat, as, *I'll baste your sides Sirrah*, I'll bang you lustily.

Bastonado-ing, a Cudgelling.

Batten, c. to Fatten.

Battner, c. an Ox.

Batter, the Ingredients for a Pudding or Pan-cake, when they are all mixt and stirred together.

Battery, beating, assault, also, striking with the Edge and *feble* of one's Sword, upon the edge and *feble* of his Adversaries.

Batter'd-bully, an old well cudgell'd and bruis'd huffing Fellow.

Baubee, a half-penny.

Baubels, c. Jewels, also trifles and Childrens Play-things.

Bawdy-baskets, c. the Twenty third Rank of Canters, with Pins, Tape, Obscene Books, *&c.* to sell, but live more by Stealing.

Bawdy-batchelors, that live long Unmarried.

Bawdy-house-bottle, a very small one.

Bay-windows, embowed, as of old, standing out from the rest of the Building. *Stand at bay*, as Deer will, when closely pursued, or being hard run, turn Head against the Hounds.

Beach, the Sea-shore, or Strand.

Bear-garden-discourse, common, filthy, nasty Talk. *If if had been a Bear it would have bit you*, of him that makes a close search after what just lies under his Nose. *As good take a Bear by the Tooth*, of a bold desperate Undertaking. *Go like the Bear to the Stake*, or hang an Arse. *As many tricks as a dancing Bear*, or more than are good.

Beard splitter, an enjoyer of Women.

Beateth, the noise a Hare makes at Rutting time.

Beating, striking the *Feble* of the Adversary's Sword, with
    the *Fort* and edge of one's own.

Beau, a silly Fellow that Follows the Fashions nicely,
    Powdering his Neck, Shoulders, *&c.*

Beautrap, a Sharper.

Beck, c. a Beedle.

Beetle-head, a heavy dull Block-head.

Beldam, a scolding old Woman.

Belle, a nice, gay, fluttring foolish Woman that follows
    every Fashion, also fair.

Belloweth, see Roe.

Belly-cheat, c. an Apron.

Belsh, all Mault drinks.

Belweather, chief or Leader of the Flock, Master of misrule,
    also a clamorous noisy Man.

Bene, c. good.

Bene-cove, c. a good Fellow.

Bene-ship, c. very good, also Worship.

Bene-bowse, c. strong Liquor, or very good Drink.

Bene-darkmans, c. good night.

Benfeakers of Gybes, c. Counterfeiters of Passes.

Benefit of Clergy, see Neck-verse.

Ben, a Fool.

Bennish, Foolish.

Beside-himself, distracted, *beside the Cushion*, a mistake, *beside
    the Lighter*, in a bad condition.

Besom, a Broom.

Bestrid, Mounted or got up astride.

Bess, c. *bring bess and glym*, forget not the Instrument to
    break open the Door and the Dark-lanthorn.

Betty, c. a small Engin to force open the Doors of Houses; also, a quarter Flask of Wine.

Bever, an afternoon's Lunchion.

Beveridge, a Garnish-money, for any thing; also Wine and Water.

Bevy, a company of Roes, Quails, &c. *Bevy Grease*, Roes fat.

Bewildred, at a stand or nonplus in Business, not knowing what to do, also lost in a Wood.

Biddy, a Chicken, also Bridget.

Big, choice Barley-making, the best Mault.

Biggin, a Woman's Coif.

Biggot, an obstinate blind Zealot.

Biggotry, an obstinate blind Zeal.

Bil-boa, c. a Sword.

Bite the Bil from the Cull c. whip the Sword from the Gentleman's side.

Bilk, c. to cheat. *Bilk the Ratling-cove*, c. to sharp the Coachman of his hire.

Bilk'd, c. defeated, disappointed.

Billeting, Foxes Excrements. *Billeting* of Soldiers, Quartering them.

Billet-doux, a Love-letter.

Bill-of-sale, a Bandore, or Widow's Peak.

Billingsgate-dialect, Scolding, ill Language, foul Words.

Binding, securing the Adversary's Sword with Eight or ten Inches of one's one, upon Five or six of his.

Bing, c. to go, &c.

Bing-awast, c. get you hence. *Bing'd awast in a Darkmans*, c. stole away in the Night-time. *Bing we to Rume vile*, c. go we to *London*.

Bingo, c. Brandy.

Bingo-boy, c. a great Drinker or Lover thereof.

Bingo-club, c. a set of *Rakes*; Lovers of that Liquor.

Birds of a Feather, c. Rogues of the same gang; also, those of the same Profession, Trade or Employment. *To kill two Brids with one Stone*, to dispatch two Businesses at one Stroke.

Bird-witted, Wild-headed, not Solid or Stayed, opposed to a Sober-Wit.

Bit, c. Robb'd, Cheated or Out-witted. Also Drunk, as, *he has bit his Grannam;* he is very Drunk. *Bit the Blow*, c. accomplish'd the Theft, plaied the Cheat, or done the Feat: *You have Bit a great Blow*, c. you have Robb'd some body of a great deal, or to a considerable value.

Bite, c. a Rogue, Sharper or Cheat; also a Womans Privities.

Bite the Biter, c. to Rob the Rogue, Sharp the Sharper, or Cheat the Cheater.

Bite the Cully, c. to put the cheat on the silly Fellow.

Bite the Roger, c. to Steal the Portmanteau. *Bite the Wiper*, c. to Steal the Hand-kerchief. *The Cull wapt the Morts bite*, c. the Fellow enjoyed the Whore briskly. *He will not bite, or swallow the Bait*. He won't be drawn in, *to bite on the bit;* to be pinched, or reduced to hard Meat, a scanty or sorry sort of Living.

Bitter-cold, very Cold.

Black and White, under one's Hand, or in Writing.

Blab, a Sieve of Secrets, a very prating Fellow that tells all he knows.

Black-box, a Lawyer.

Black-coat, a Parson.

Black-guard, Dirty, Nasty, Tatter'd roguish Boys, that

attend (at the Horse-Guards) to wipe Shoes, clean Boots, water Horses, or run of Errands.

Blackjack, a Leather-Jug to drink in.

Black-Indies, Newcastle, from whence the Coals are brought.

Blackmuns, c. Hoods and Scarves of Alamode and Lustrings.

Black-mouth, foul, malicious, Railing, or Reflecting.

Blacken, to blast or asperse.

Black-spy, c. the Devil.

Blank, baffled, down-look't, sheepish, guilty.

Bleak, sharp, piercing Weather.

Bleach, to whiten.

Bleaters, c. they that are cheated by Jack-in-a box.

Bleating cheat, c. a Sheep.

Bleed freely, c. part with their Money easily.

Blemish, when Hounds or Beagles find where the Chace has been, and make a proffer to enter, but return.

Blew-John, Wash, or Afterwort.

Blind-cheeks, the Breech. *Kiss my Blind-cheeks*, Kiss my Ar——.

Blind-excuse, a sorry shift. *A Blind Ale-house, or Blind Lane*, obscure, of no Sign, Token, or Mark.

Blind-harpers, c. Beggars counterfeiting blindness, with Harps or Fiddles.

Blind-man's-buff, a play us'd by Children blind-folded. *Bluffed*, contracted from Blind-man's-buff, he that is Blinded in the Play.

Blind-man's-holiday, when it is too dark to see to Work.

Blind side, every Man's weak Part.

Bloated, Smoked Herrings; also, one puffed or swelled with false Fat, and has not a Healthy Complexion.

Blobber-lipp'd, very thick, hanging down, or turning over.

Block, a silly Fellow.

Block-houses, c. Prisons, also Forts upon Rivers.

Blockish, Stupid.

Blockstock, See Block.

Bloss, c. a Thief or Shop-lift, also, a Bullies pretended Wife, or Mistress, whom he guards, and who by her Trading supports him, also a Whore.

Blot the Skrip and jark it, c. to stand Engaged, or be Bound for any body.

Blot in the Tables, what is fair to be hit.

Blot in a Scutcheon, a blemish or imputation upon any one.

Bloud, *'twill breed ill Bloud*, of what will produce a misunderstanding or Difference.

Blower, c. a Mistress, also a Whore.

Blowing, c. *the same*.

Blow-off-on the groun-sills, c. to lie with a Woman on the Floor or Stairs.

Blown upon, seen by several, or slighted; *not blown upon*, a secret piece of News or Poetry, that has not taken air, spick and span-new. *To blow Hot and Cold* with a Breath, or play fast and loose.

Blow off the loose corns, c. to Lie now and then with a Woman. *It is blow'd*, c. it is made publick, and all have notice.

Blubber, Whale-oyl, (imperfect.)

Blubbering, much Crying.

Bluffer, c. a Host, Inn-keeper or Victualler, *to look bluff*, to look big, or like Bull-beef.

Blunder, an Ignorant Mistake.

Blunderbuss, a Dunce, an unganely Fellow, also a short Gun carrying Twenty Pistol-Bullets at one Charge.

Bluster, to huff, *a blustring Fellow*, a rude ratling Fellow.

Boar, see wild Boar.

Boarding-school, c. Bridewell.

Boarding-scholars, c. Bridewell-birds.

Bob, c. a Shop-lift's camrade, assistant, or receiver, also a very short Periwig, and for Robert. *It's all bob*, c. all is safe, the Bet is secured.

Bob'd, c. Cheated, Trick'd, Disappointed, or Baulk'd.

Bob-tail, a light Woman, also a short Arrow-head.

Bode-ill, to presage or betoken ill. Also in *Holland*, a *Bode* is a Messinger, attending the Burgo-Masters, and executing their Orders.

Bodle, Six make a Penney, Scotch Coin.

Boer, a Country-Fellow or Clown.

Boerish, Rude, Unmannerly, Clownish.

Boggs, Irish Fastnesses or Marshes.

Bog-houses, Privies.

Bog-landers, Irish Men.

Bog-trotters, Scotch or North Country Moss-troopers or High-way Men formerly, and now Irish Men.

Boisterous Fellow or, *Sea*, Blustering, Rude, Rough.

Boldface, Impudent. A *Bold Harbour*, where Ships may Ride at Anchor with safety, *a bold Shore* where Ships may Sail securely.

Bolter of White Friers, c. one that Peeps out, but dares not venture abroad, as a Coney bolts out of the Hole in a Warren, and starts back again.

Bolting, the leaping by one's Adversary's Left-side quite out of all measure.

Boltsprit, a Nose. *He has broke his Boltsprit*, he has lost his Nose with the Pox.

Bombast-poetry, in Words of lofty Sound and humble Sense.

Bone, c. to Apprehend, Seize, Take or Arrest. *I'll Bone ye*, c. I'll cause you to be Arrested. *We shall be Bon'd*, c. we shall be Apprehended for the Robbery. *The Cove is Bon'd and gon to the Whit*, c. the Rogue is taken up and carried to Newgate, or any other Goal. *The Cull has Bon'd the Fen*, (for *Fence*) or *Bloss that bit the Blow*, c. the Man has Taken the Thief that Robb'd his House, Shop, or Pickt his Pocket. *He has bit his Blow, but if he be Bon'd, he must shove the Tumbler*, c. he has Stole the Goods, or done the Feat, but if he be Taken, he'll be Whipt at the Cart-tail. *I have Bon'd her Dudds, Fagg'd, and Brush'd*, c. I have took away my Mistress Cloathes, Beat her, and am troop'd off. *Boning the Fence*, c. finding the Goods where Conceal'd, and Seizing, *he made no bones of it*, he swallow'd it without Drinking after it.

Bonny-clapper, sower Butter-milk.

Booby, a dull heavy Lob.

Booberkin, the same.

Boon, a Gift, Reward, or Gratification.

Boon-companion, a merry Drinking Fellow.

Boot, a Scotch Torture, or Rack, for the Leg, is to draw to Confession.

What Boots it? What Avails it?

Booty-play, False, Cheating, also Plunder, he *Bowls Booty*, when great Odds are laid, and he goes Halves, his Cast is designed by Bad.

Boracho, A But, a Drunkard, and a Hogskin.

Borde, c. a Shilling, *half a Borde*, c. Sixpence.

Bordel-lo, a Bawdy-House.

Boreson or *Bauson*, a Badger.

Bottle-head, void of Wit.

Bottom, *a Man of no Bottom*, of no Basis of Principles, or no settlement of Fortune, or of no Ground in his Art. *Let every Tub stand on it's own Bottom*, or every one look to his own footing. *A Tale of a Tub with the Bottom out*, a sleeveless frivolous Tale.

Boughs, *he is up in the Boughs*, *or a top of the House*, of one upon the Rant, or in a great Ferment.

Bounce, to boast and vapour. *A meer Bounce*, a Swaggering Fellow.

Bouncer, c. a Bully.

Bout, a Tryal, Act, Essay.

Bowse, c. Drink, or to Drink, see *Benbowse* and *Rumbowse*.

Bowsy. c. Drunk. *We Bows'd it about*, we Drank damn'd hard.

Bowsingken, c. an Ale-house. *The Cul tipt us a Hog*, *which we melted in Rumbowse*, c. the Gentleman gave us a Shilling, which we spent in Strong Drink.

Box, to Fight with the Fists. *Box it about Boys*, Drink briskly round. *In a wrong Box*, of one that has taken wrong measures, or made false steps. *A pretty Box*, a Compleat little House, also a small drinking place.

Bracket-face, Ugly, Homely, Ill favor'd.

Bragget, Meed, and Ale sweetned with Honey.

Brag, *Braggadocio*, A vapouring, Swaggering, Bullying Fellow.

Brat, a little Child.

Branchers, Canary-Birds of the first Year.

Bravado, a Vapouring, or Bouncing.

Bravo, a Mercenary Murderer, that will Kill any Body.

Brawl, Squabble, or Quarrel. *To Brangle*, *and Brawl*, to Squabble and Scold.

Brazen-fac'd, Bold, Impudent, Audacious.

Bread and Cheese Bowling-green, a very ord'nary one, where they play for Drink and Tobacco, all wet, as 'tis called.

Bread and Cheese Constables, that treats their Neighbors and Friends at their coming into Office with such mean Food only.

Breaking Shins, c. borrowing of Money.

Breast, in the breast of the Judge, what he keeps in Reserve, or Suspence.

Briers, in the Briers, in trouble.

Brook, he cannot brook it, bear or endure it.

Brickle, Brittle, apt to Break.

Bristol-milk, Sherry.

Bristol-stone, Sham-Diamonds.

Broach'd, Opinion or Doctrine, Published, Divulged.

Brimming, a Boor's copulating with a Sow, also now us'd for a Man's with—

Brim, or *Brimstone*, a very Impudent, Lew'd Woman.

Brock, see Hart.

Brock's Sister, see Hind.

Broke, Officers turn'd out of Commission, Traders Absconding, Quitting their Business and Paying no Debts.

Bromigham-conscience, very bad, *Bromigham-protestants*, Dissenters or Whiggs. *Bromigham-wine*, Balderdash, Sophisticate Taplash.

Brother-starling, that Lies with the same Woman, or Builds in the same Nest.

Brother of the { *Blade*, a Sword-Man or Soldier.
Gussit, a Pimp, Procurer, also, a Whore-Master.
Quill, of the Scribbling Tribe.
String, a Fidler, or Musician.

Brothel-house, a Bawdy House.

Brow-beat, to Cow, to Daunt, to awe with Big Looks, or Snub.

Brown-study, a Deep Thought or Speculation.

Brush, c. to Fly or Run away. *The Cully is Brusht or Rub'd*, c. the Fellow is march'd off, or Broke. *Bought a Brush*, c. Run away: Also a small Faggot, to light the other at Taverns, and a Fox's Tail.

Brusher, c. an exceeding full Glass.

Bub, c. Drink. *Rum-bub*, c. very good Tip.

Bub, or *Bubble*, c. one that is Cheated; also an Easy, Soft Fellow.

Bubber, c. a drinking Bowl; also a great Drinker, and he that used to Steal Plate from Publick-houses.

Bube, c. the Pox. *The Mort has tipt the Bube upon the Cully*, c. the Wench has Clapt the Fellow.

Buckaneers, West-Indian Pirates, of several Nations; also the Rude Rabble in Jamaica.

Buckle, to Bend or give Way. *He'll buckle to no Man*, he won't Yield or Stoop to any Man.

Buck, *Great Buck*, the Sixth Year. *Buck of the first Head*, the Fifth Year, a *Sore*, the Fourth Year, a *Sorel*, the Third Year, a *Pricket*, the Second Year, a *Fawn*, the First Year. *A Buck Lodgeth. Rouze the Buck*, Dislodge him. *A Buck Growneth or Troateth*, makes a Noise at Rutting time.

Buck-fitches, c. old Leacherous, Nasty, Stinking Fellows; also He Polecats, and their Fur.

Buck's Face, a Cuckold.

Buck, Copulation of Conies.

Bucksom, Wanton, Merry.

Budge, c. one that slips into an House in the Dark, and

taketh Cloaks, Coats, or what comes next to Hand, marching off with them; also Lambs-fur, and to stir, or move. *Standing Budge*, c. the Thieves Scout or Perdu.

Bufe, c. a Dog.

Buffcoat, a Soldier, or Redcoat.

Buffer, c. a Rogue that kills good sound Horses, only for their Skins, by running a long Wyre into them, and sometimes knocking them on the Head, for the quicker Dispatch.

Buffenapper, c. a Dog-stealer, that Trades in *Setters*, *Hounds*, *Spaniels*, *Lap*, and all sorts of Dogs, Selling them at a round Rate, and himself or Partner Stealing them away the first opportunity.

Buffers-nab, c. a Dog's Head, used in a Counterfeit Seal to a false Pass.

Buffle-head, a Foolish Fellow.

Buffoon, a Great Man's Jester or Fool.

Buffoonery, Jesting or playing the Fool's Part. *To stand Buff*, to stand Tightly or Resolutely to any thing.

Bugher, c. a Dog.

Bugging, c. taking Money by Bailiffs and Serjeants of the Defendant not to Arrest him.

Busy-bodies, Fryers into other Folks Concerns, such as thrust their Sickle in another's Harvest; and will have an Oar in every Boat. *As Busy as a Hen with one Chick*, of one that has a great deal of business and nothing to do.

Bulchim, a Chubbingly Boy or Lad.

Bulls-Eye, c. a Crown or Five shilling Piece.

Bull-head, see Miller's Thumb.

Bull, an absurd contradiction or incongruity; also false Hair worn (formerly much) by Women. *A Town-bull*, a Whore-master. *To look like Bull-beef*, to look Big and Grim.

Bulk and File, c. one jostles while the other Picks the Pocket.

Bulker, c. one that lodges all Night on Shop-windows and Bulkheads.

Bulky, strong like common Oyl, also of large bulk or size.

Bullet-headed, a dull silly Fellow.

Bully, c. a supposed Husband to a Bawd, or Whore; also a huffing Fellow.

Bully huff, c. a poor sorry Rogue that haunts Bawdy-houses, and pretends to get Money out of Gentlemen and others, Ratling and Swearing the Whore is his Wife, calling to his assistance a parcel of Hectors.

Bully-fop, c. a Maggot-pated, huffing, silly ratling Fellow.

Bully-rock, c. a Hector, or Bravo.

Bully-ruffins, c. Highway-men, or Padders.

Bully-trap, c. or *Trapan*, c. a Sharper, or Cheat.

Bum, a Bailiff, or Serjeant, also one's Breech.

Bumbast, see Bombast.

Bumbaste, to Beat much, or hard, on the Breech.

Bumble, Cloaths setting in a heap, or ruck.

Bumfodder, what serves to wipe the Tail.

Bumpkin, a Country Fellow or Clown.

Bumper, a full Glass.

Bundletail, a short Fat or squat Lass.

Bungler, an unperforming Husband, or Mechanic.

Bung, c. a Purse, Pocket, or Fob.

Bung-nipper, c. a Cut-purse, or Pickpocket. *Claying the Bung*, c. cutting the Purse, or Picking the Pocket.

Bunting-time, when the Grass is high enough to hide the young Men and Maids.

Buntlings, c. Pettycoats. *Hale up the Main-buntlings*, c. take up the Woman's Pettycoats.

Bunny, a Rabbit.

Bur, a Cloud, or dark Circle about the Moon, boding Wind and Rain; also the part next to the Deer's Head.

Burlesque, Raillery in Verse, or Verse in Ridicule.

Burnish, to spread, or grow broad; also to refresh Plate, being the Trade of a

Burnisher, depending on Gold and Silver-Smiths.

Burnt, Poxt, or swingingly Clapt.

Burnt the Town, when the Soldiers leave the Place without paying their Quarters.

Burre, a Hanger on, or Dependant.

Bustle, a Fray, Stir, Tumult in the Streets; also a Noise in any Place. *What a Bustle you make?* What a Hurry or Rattle you Cause? *Bustle about*, to be very Stirring, or bestir one's Stumps.

Butcher'd, Barbarously Murder'd on the Ground, or Kill'd before his Sword is out; also in Cold Bloud.

Butter, c. to double or treble the Bet or Wager to recover all Losses. *No Butter will stick on his Bread*, nothing thrives or goes forward in his Hand. *He knows on which side his Bread is Butter'd*, or the Stronger side, and his own Interest.

Butter-boxes, Dutchmen.

Butter'd Bun, Lying with a Woman that has been just Layn with by another Man.

Buttock, c. a Whore.

Buttock-broker, a Bawd, also a Match-maker. *A Buttock and File*, c. both Whore and Pickpocket.

Buttock and Twang, or a downright Buttock and sham File, c. a Common Whore but no Pickpocket.

Buzzard, c. a foolish soft Fellow, easily drawn in and Cullied or Trickt.

By-blow, a Bastard.

C

Cabal, a secret Junto of Princes, a seated knot of Statesmen, or of Conspirators against the State in Counter-Cabal.

Cabbage, a Taylor and what they pinch from the Cloaths they make up; also that part of the Deer's Head where the Horns are Planted.

Cabob, a Loin of Mutton Roasted with an Onyon betwixt each joint; a *Turkish* and *Persian* Dish but now used in *England*.

Cacafuego, a Shite-fire; also a furious fierce Fellow.

Cackle, c. to discover. *The Cull Cackles*, c. the Rogue tells all.

Cackling-cheats, c. Chickens, Cocks or Hens.

Cackling-farts, c. Eggs.

Cadet, or *Cadee*, a Gentleman that Bears Arms in hopes of a Commission; also a younger Brother.

Caffan, c. Cheese.

Cakehis, *Cake is Dough*, of a Miscarriage or failure of Business. *The Devil ow'd her a Cake, and has pai'd her a Loaf*, when instead of a small, a very great Disaster, or Misfortune has happen'd to a Woman.

Call, a Lesson, Blowed on the Horn to comfort the Hounds.

Caliver, a small Sea-Gun.

Calle, c. a Cloak or Gown.

Cambridge-Fortune, a Woman without any Substance.

Cameleon-Diet, Air, or a very thin slender Diet.

Cameronians, Field Conventiclers, (in *Scotland*) great
outward Zealots, and very squeemish Precisians.

Camesa, c. a Shirt or Shift.

Campaign-coat, Originally only such as Soldiers wore, but
afterwards a Mode in Cities. See *Surtout*.

Canary-Bird, a little Arch or Knavish, a very Wag.

Cane upon Abel, a good Stick or Cudgel well-favoredly laid
on a Man's Shoulders.

Canal, a Channel, Kennel, Pipe, Passage, fine Pond, or small
River.

Cannal, choice Coals, very Fat or Pitchy that Blaze and
Burn pleasantly.

Canibal, a cruel rigid Fellow in dealing; also Men-Eaters.

Cank, c. Dumb. *The Cull's Cank*, c. the Rogue's Dumb.

Cannikin, c. the Plague, also (among the *Dutch*) a little Kan
with a Spout to pour out the Wine or Beer, making it
Froth. *As great as Cup and Cann*; or *as great as two
Inkle-makers*.

Cant, c. to speak, also (Cheshire) to grow Strong and
Lusty; also to Kick or throw any thing away.

Canterbury, a sort of a short or Hand-gallop; from the Road
leading to that famous City (of *Kent*) on which they
Ride (for the most part) after that manner.

Canting, c. the Cypher or Mysterious Language, of Rogues,
Gypsies, Beggers, Thieves, *&c.*

Canting-crew, c. Beggers, Gypsies; also Dissenters in
Conventicles, who affect a disguised Speech, and

disguised Modes of Speaking, and distinguish
themselves from others by a peculiar Snuffle and Tone,
as the Shibboleth of their Party; as Gypsies and Beggers
have their peculiar Jargon; and are known no less by
their several Tones in Praying, than Beggers are by
their whining Note in Begging.

Cap, c. to Swear. *I'll Cap downright*, c. I'll Swear home. Or
(in another Sense) *he may fling up his Cap after it*, when a
thing or business is past Hope.

Capitation-Drugget, a Cheap, Slight Stuff, called so from the
Tax of that Name.

Capricious, Whimsical, Fantastic, Freakish.

Captain-Hackum, c. a Fighting, Blustring Bully.

Captain-Queere nabs, c. a Fellow in poor Cloths, or Shabby.

Captain-sharp, c. a great Cheat; also a Huffing, yet Sneaking,
Cowardly Bully; and a noted English Buckaneer.

Captain-Tom, a Leader of, and the Mob.

Captious, Touchy, Snuffy, apt to take Exception.

Caravan, c. a good round sum of Money about a Man, and
him that is Cheated of it; also a great Convoy of
Arabian, *Grecian*, *Persian*, *Turkish*, and other Merchants,
Travelling with Camels from Place to Place; also a sort
of Wagon.

Carbuncle-Face, very Red and full of large Pimples.

Card-Wool, to cleanse and prepare it for Spinning: Also a
Game; *a sure Card*, a trusty Tool, or Confiding Man; a
cooling Card, cold comfort, no hope; *a Leading Card*, an
Example or Precedent.

Cargo, c. a good round Sum of Money about a Man; also the
Lading of a Ship.

Carouse, to Drink hard, or Quaff heartily.

Carpet-road. Level and very good.

Carriers, Pigeons that will with safety, and almost incredible Swiftness convey Letters from one Place to another, much used at *Smyrna* and *Aleppo*; also Milk-womens Hirelings, or Servants, that carry the Pail Morning and Evening.

Carrots, Red hair'd People, from the Colour of the well known Root of that Name, whence came

Carrot-pated, used in derision.

Carted-Whore, Whipt publicly, and packt out of Town. *The Cart before the Horse,* of a thing preposterous, and out of Place.

Cash, c. Cheese.

Case, c. a House, Shop, or Ware-house; also a Bawdy-house. *Toute the Case,* c. to view, mark, or eye the House or Shop. *There's a peerey, 'tis snitch,* c. there are a great many People, there's no good to be don. *'Tis all Bob, and then to dub the gigg,* c, now the coast is clear, there's good Booty, let's fall on, and Rob the House. *A Case fro,* c. a Whore that Plies in a Bawdy-house.

Caster, c. a Cloak.

Cast, to Bowl. *A bad cast,* an ill laid Bowl, or at great distance from the Jack. *He is Cast for Felon and Dose,* c. found guilty of Felony and Burglary.

Cat, a common Whore or Prostitute.

Catch-fart, a Foot-Boy.

Catching-harvest, when the Weather is Showery and Unsettled.

Catch-pole, a Serjeant, or Bayliff that Arrests People.

Cat-in-pan, turn'd, of one that has chang'd Sides or Parties. *Who shall hang the Bell about the Cat's Neck,* said of a desperate Undertaking.

Catchup, a high *East-India* Sauce.

Caterwauling, Men and Women desirous of Copulation, a
Term borrowed from Cats.

Cathedral, old-fashioned, out of Date, Ancient; also a chief
Church in a Bishop's See.

Catharpin-fashion, when People in Company Drink cross,
and not round about from the Right to the Left, or
according to the Sun's motion; also small Ropes to keep
the Shrouds, taut or tight, and the Mast from Rolling.

Catting, drawing a Fellow through a Pond with a Cat.

Catstick, used by Boies at Trap-ball.

Cattle, Whores. *Sad Cattle*, Impudent Lewd Women.

Catmatch, c. when a Rook is Engag'd amongst bad Bowlers.

Cavalcade, a publick Show on Horseback.

Cavaulting School, c. a Bawdy-house.

Caudge-paw'd, Left Handed.

Caveating, or *Disengaging*, slipping the Adversary's Sword,
when 'tis going to bind or secure one's own.

Caw-handed, awkward not dextrous, ready or nimble.

Changeable-ribbon, or *Silks*, of diverse Colours, resembling
those of Doves-necks, or of the *Opal* Stone.

Chafe, *in a great Chafe*, great heat or pet. *To Chafe*, to fret or
fume, fretting or fuming, *Chafing and fretting*, being the
same with fretting and fuming, hence a

Chafing dish, that carries Fire.

Chaft, c. well beaten or bang'd; also much rub'd or bath'd.

Chagrin, moody, out of humour, pensive, melancholy, much
troubled.

Chalk, used in Powder by the Perfumers to mix with their
Grounds; and also scented Hair-Powders, being cheap
and weighing heavy; found to Burn and destroy Wiggs
and all Hair in general.

Chanticlere, a Cock.

Chape, the Tip at the End of a Fox's Tail; also the Cap at the End of the Scabbard of a Sword.

Character, a distinguishing Sign or Mark of Distinction, the same among Great Men or Ministers, that a Badge is among Low and little People. *As a Man of Character*, of Mark or Note, as Privy-Chancellors, Judges, Foreign Ministers, Ministers of State, *&c.*

Chare-women, Under-drudges, or Taskers, assistants to Servantmaids.

Char, a Task or Work. *A good Char well Char'd*, a Work well over.

Chates, c. the Gallows.

Chat, Talk, Prate.

Chatter, to Talk fast or jabber.

Chattering Fellow, a noisy prating Man.

Chatts, c. Lice. *Squeeze the Chatts*, c. to Crack or Kill those Vermin.

Cheap, Contemptible. *How Cheap you make your self*, how Contemptible you render your self or undervalue your self.

Chear, good or *bad*, high or ordinary fare. *How Chear you?* How fare you? *Chear up*, be of good courage, hence *chearful*, or *chearly*, for one in Heart, or that keeps up his Spirits: *prety chearly*, indifferent hearty or lightsom.

Cheats, Sharpers, which see; also Wristbands or sham Sleeves worn (in good Husbandry) for true, or whole ones.

Chicken, a feeble, little creature, of mean Spirit; whence *a Chicken-hearted Fellow*, or *Hen-hearted Fellow*, a Dastard.

Childish, Foolish.

Childing-women, Breeding.

China-Ale, From the well known *East-Indian* Drug of that Name, of which they ought to put some, but they seldom do any into it, making it sweet only and adding a little Spice.

Chink, c. Money, because it chinks in the Pocket.

Chip, a Child.

Chip of the old Block, a Son that is his Father's likeness; more particularly the Son of a Cooper, or one brought up to the same Trade.

Chirping-merry, very pleasant over a Glass of good Liquor.

Chit, a Dandyprat, or Dergen.

Chittiface, a little puiny Child.

Chitchat, idle Prate, or empty Talk.

Chive, c. a Knife.

Chop, to change, or barter.

Chopping-boy, a bouncing Boy. *To chop up Prayers*, to huddle them up, or slubber them over in posthast. *A Chop by chance*, a rare Contingence, an extraordinary or uncommon Event; out of course.

Chopps, (of a Man) his Face (of Mutton) a Bone or Cut.

Chounter, to talk pertly, and (sometimes) angrily.

Chouse, to cheat or trick.

Chop-houses, where Both boy'd and roast Mutton (in chopps) are always ready.

Chub, c. *he is a young chub, or a meer chub*, c. very ignorant or inexperienc'd in gaming, not at all acquainted with Sharping. *A good Chub*, said by the Butchers; when they have met with a silly raw Customer, and they have Bit him.

Chuck-farthing, a Parish-Clerk (in the Satyr against Hypocrites); also a Play among Boies.

Chum, a Chamber-fellow, or constant Companion.

Church-yard-cough, that will terminate in Death.

Churl, an Ill-natur'd Fellow; a selfish, sordid Clown. *To put a Churl upon a Gentleman*, to Drink Ale or any Mault-Liquor immediately after Wine.

Ciento, an old Game at Cards.

Citt, for Citizen.

Civil List, all the Officers and Servants in the King's Family.

Clack, a Woman's Tongue.

Clammed, Starved, or Famished.

Clan, Family, Tribe, Faction, Party in *Scotland* chiefly, but now any where else.

Clank, c. a Silver-tankard. *Clanker*, a swinging Lie.

Clank-napper, c. a Silver-tankard Stealer. See *Bubber*, *Rum-clank*, c. a large Silver-tankard. *Tip me a rum Clank a Booz*, c. give me a double Tankard of Drink.

Clap, a Venereal Taint.

Clapperclaw'd, beat soundly, or paid off in earnest.

Clapperdogeon, c. a Begger-born and Bred.

Clark, or *Clerk*, Scholar or Book-learned.

Clerk-ship, or *Clergy*, Scholarship or Book-learning, though of late the one be more restrained to a Clergyman, and the other appropriate to a Clergyman's Skill or Qualifications; because it may be heretofore, none but the Clergy were learned, or so much as taught to Read. Hence, *the Benefit of Clergy*, (or Reading) *& legit ut Clericus*, in the Law, for him that cou'd Read his Neck-verse, like a Clerk or Scholar, when so few perhaps were Scholars or Clerks, that every one that could but only Read, passed for no less: We say still, the greatest Clarks (or Scholars) are not the Wisest Men: And the

Scots much to the same Effect. An Ounce of Mother-
Wit is worth a Pound of Clergy, or Book-learning.

Claw'd off, lustily lasht, also swingingly Poxt.

Clear, c. very Drunk. *The Cull is clear, let's Bite him*, c. The
Fellow is Damn'd Drunk, let's Sharp him.

Cleave, has two contrary Senses under one Sound; for *to
cleave*, (Verb Neuter) is to cling close or stick fast, and *to
cleave*, (verb Active) is to part or divide; as to cleave
asunder, when *Cleft* and *Cloven*.

Clench, a pun or quible; also to nick a Business by timing it.

Cleymes, c. Sores without Pain raised on Beggers Bodies, by
their own Artifice and cunning, (to move charity) by
bruising Crows-foot, Speerwort and salt together, and
clapping them on the Place, which frets the Skin, then
with a Linnen rag, which sticks close to it; they tear off
the Skin, and strew on it a little Powder'd Arsnick,
which makes it look angrily or ill favoredly, as if it were
a real Sore.

Click, c. to Snatch. *I have Clickt the Nab from the Cull*, c. I
whipt the Hat from the Man's Head. *Click the rum
Topping*, c. Snatch that Woman's fine Commode.

Clicker, the Shoe-maker's Journey-man, or Servant, that
Cutts out all the Work, and stands at or walks before
the Door, and saies, what d'ye' lack Sir, what d'ye buy
Madam.

Clicket, Copulation of Foxes, and sometimes, used waggishly
for that of Men and Women.

Clinker, c. a crafty Fellow.

Clinkers, c. the Irons Felons wear in Goals.

Clip, to hug or embrace. *To clip and cling*, of a close hug or
fast embrace. *To Clip the Coin*, to diminish or Impair it.

To clip the Kings English, not to Speak Plain, when one's Drunk.

Clod-hopper, c. a Plough-man.

Clodpate, a heavy, dull Fellow.

Close, reserv'd, silent, not talkative, or open.

Close-confident, a trusty Bosom-friend.

Close-fisted, covetous, stingy, pinching.

Clotts, or thick dropps of Bloud clottered or in clots.

Cloud, c. Tobacco. *Will ye raise a Cloud*, c. Shall we Smoke a Pipe?

Clouds, or *Cloudy-Sky*, in opposition to clear open Sky; as *Clouds in Gemms and Stones*, to clear ones; and *Clouded Face*, to a clear pleasant one. *Under a Cloud*, in disgrace, under misfortunes or disasters; *Speaks in the Clouds*, of one that flies or soars in Talking above the common reach or capacity.

Cloudy, dark complexion d.

Clout, c. a Handkerchief.

Cloy, c. to Steal. *Cloy the Clout*, c. to Steal the Hankerchief. *Cloy the Lour*, c. to Steal the Money; also, in another Sense, *to Cloy*, is to Nauseate or Satiate.

Cloyers, c. Thieves, Robbers, Rogues.

Cloying, c. Stealing, Thieving, Robbing; also Fulsom or Satiating.

Clowes, c. Rogues.

Clown, a Country-Fellow, also one very Ill-bred or unmannerly, Being.

Clownish, rustical, unpolish'd, uncouth.

Club, each Man's particular Shot; also a Society of Men agreeing to meet according to a Scheme of Orders under a slight Penalty to promote Trade and Friendship.

Cluck, the noise made by Hens, when they set upon their Eggs to Hatch and are disturb'd, or come off to Eat, and also when they wou'd have Eggs put under them for that purpose.

Clump, a Heap or Lump.

Clunch, a clumsy Clown, an awkward or unhandy Fellow.

Clutch the Fist, or close the Hand, whence *Clutches*. *I'll keep out of your Clutches or Claws*; *the Clutches of the Parish*, the Constable or Beadle.

Clutchfisted, the same as Closefisted.

Clutter, Stir. *What a Clutter you keep?* What a stir you make?

Cly, c. Money. *To Cly the Jerk*, c. to be Whipt. *Let's strike his Cly*, c. let's get his Money from him; also a Pocket, *Filed a cly*, c. Pickt a Pocket.

Coach-wheel { *Fore* { Half a Crown. { *Hind* { A Crown or Five Shilling-Piece.

Coals to Newcastle when the Drawer carries away any Wine in the Pot or Bottle. *To blow the Coals*, to raise differences between Parties. *He'll carry no Coals*, not be Pissed upon, or Imposed upon, nor bear a Trick, or take an Affront, or tamely pass by any ill Treatment. *Let him that has need blow the Coals*, Let him Labour that wants.

Cob, a Dollar (in Ireland).

Cobble, to mend or patch.

Cobbled, bunglingly done.

Cobble-colter, c. a Turkey. *A rum Cobble-colter*, c. a fat large Cock-Turkey.

Cobweb-cheat, easily found out.

Cobweb-pretence, slight, trivial, weak.

Cock-a-hoop, upon the high Ropes Rampant, Transported.

Cockish, wanton uppish, forward.

Cockale, pleasant Drink, said to be provocative.

Cock-baw'd, Man that follows that base Employment.

Cocker, one skill'd in, or much delighted with the sport of Cock-fighting.

Cockney, Born within the Sound of Bow-bell; (in *London*) also one ignorant in Country Matters.

Cock-oyster, the Male.

Cock-pimp, a Supposed Husband to a Bawd.

Cock-robbin, a soft easy Fellow.

Cock-sure, very Sure.

Cod, a good sum of Money; also a Fool. *A meer Cod*, a silly, shallow Fellow. *A rum Cod*, c. a good round sum of Money. *A jolly or lusty Cod*, c. the same. *An honest Cod*, a trusty Friend.

Codders, gatherers of Peascods.

Cod's Head, a Fool.

Codsounds, the Pith or Marrow in the Cod's Back, esteem'd as choice Peck.

Cofe, c. as Cove.

Cog, to cheat at Dice. *Cog a Die*, to conceal or secure a Die; also the Money or whatever the *Sweetners* drop to draw in the Bubbles; also to wheedle, as *Cog a Dinner*, to wheedle a Spark out of a Dinner.

Cogue, of Brandy, a small Cup or Dram.

Coker, c. a Lye, *rum Coker*, c. a whisking Lye.

Cokes, the Fool in the Play, or Bartholomew-Fair, and hence (perhaps) Coxcomb.

Cold, shy, or averse to Act.

Cold-Tea, Brandy. *A couple of cold words*, a Curtain-Lecture. *Cold-Iron*, Derisory Periphrasis for a Sword. *In cold*

Blood, when the heat of War, or Passion are over. *The Matter will keep cold*, it will stay a while, and not be the worse for keeping.

Cole, c. Money.

Coliander-seed, c. Money.

Collation, a Treat or Entertainment.

College, c. Newgate; also the Royal Exchange.

Collegiates, c. those Prisoners, and Shop-keepers.

Collogue, wheedle.

Colquarron, c. a Man's Neck.

Colt, c. an Inn-keeper that lends a Horse to a Highway-man, or to Gentlemen Beggers; also a Lad newly bound Prentice.

Coltish, said when an old Fellow is frolicksom or wanton; or he has a Colt's Tooth.

Colt-bowl, laid short of the Jack by a

Colt-bowler, a raw or unexperienc'd Person.

Colt-veal, very red.

Come, c. to Lend. *Has he come it?* c. has he lent it you?

Comical, very pleasant, or diverting.

Coming-women, such as are free of their Flesh; also breeding Women.

Commission, c. a Shirt.

Commode, a Woman's Head-dress, easily put on, and as soon taken off.

Common-garden-gout, or rather Covent-garden, the Pox.

Common Women, Whores, Plyers in the Streets and at Bawdy-Houses.

Complement, the Ship's or Regiment's compleat Number or Company.

Comfortable Importance, a Wife.

Conceited, a Self-lover, and Admirer, Wise in his own Opinion.

Coney-sitteth.

Confect, c. Counterfeit.

Conger, a Set or Knot of Topping Book-sellers of *London*, who agree among themselves, that whoever of them Buys a good Copy, the rest are to take off such a particular number, as (it may be) Fifty, in Quires, on easy Terms. Also they that joyn together to Buy either a Considerable, or Dangerous Copy. And a great overgrown Sea-Eel.

Conjurers, *Astrologers*, *Physiognomists*, *Chiromancers*, and the whole Tribe of Fortune-tellers, by the common People (Ignorantly) so called.

Consent, Leave, Approbation, Agreement. *Affected by Consent*, as one Sore Eye infects the other, (unseen) because they are both strung with one Optic Nerve: As in two Strings set to an Unison, upon the Touch of One, the other will Sound.

Consult of Physicians, Two, or more.

Content, a thick Liquor, made up in Rolls in imitation of Chocolate, Sold in some Coffee-Houses.

Contre-temps, making a Pass or Thrust without any advantage, or to no purpose.

Convenient, c. a Mistress; also a Whore.

Conveniency, c. a Wife; also a Mistress.

Conundrums, Whimms, Maggots, and such like.

Cony, a silly Fellow, *a meer Cony*, very silly indeed.

Cook-ruffin, c. the Devil of a Cook, or a very bad one.

Cool-crape, a slight Chequer'd Stuff made in imitation of Scotch Plad.

Cooler, a Woman.

Cool-Lady, a Wench that sells Brandy (in Camps).

Cool-nantz, Brandy.

Cool Tankard, Wine and Water, with a Lemon Sugar and Nutmeg.

Copper-nos'd, extremely Red.

Coquet, a flippant, pert Gossip.

Corky-brain'd Fellow, silly, foolish.

Corinthian, a very impudent, harden'd, brazen-fac'd Fellow.

Cornish-hug, a hard gripe, or squeeze.

Corn-jobber, an Enhancer of the Price, by early buying, monopolizing, and sharp tricks. *A great Harvest of a little Corn*, a great adoe in a little Matter. *He measures my Corn by his own Bushel*, *he muses as he uses*, he thinks me Bad because he is so himself.

Cornuted, made a Cuckold of.

Corny-fac'd, a very Red or Blue pimpled Phiz.

Cosset, a Fondling Child.

Cosset-Colt or Lamb, brought up by Hand, made Tame, and used to follow any Body about the House.

Costard, the Head. *I'll give ye a knock on the Costard*, I'll hit ye a blow on the Pate.

Coster-monger, a Whole-sale Dealer in Apples, Pears, *&c*.

Cot for *Cotquean*, a Man that meddles with Womens matters.

Cotton, *they don't cotton*, they don't agree well.

Cote, a sorry, slight Country-House or Hovel, now a *Cottage*. Hence the Compounds yet in use, of *Dove-cote*, *Sheepcote*, *&c*.

Couchée, going to Bed. *I was at Court at the Couchee*, I attended the King at his going to Bed.

Couch a Hog's-head, c. to go to Bed.

Cove, c. a Man, a Fellow, also a Rogue. *The Cove was bit*, c. the Rogue was out-sharp'd or out-witted. *The Cove has bit the Cole*. c. The Rogue has Stolen the Money. *The Cove's a rum Diver*, c. that Fellow is a cleaver Pick-pocket.

Covey of Whores, a well fill'd Bawdy-house; also of *Partridges*, a Nest or Brood.

Counterfeit-cranks, c . the Twentieth Rank or Order of the Canting Tribe.

Counterfeit, a Cheat or Impostor. *A Counterfeiter of Hands*, a Forger. *A Counterfeiter of Persons*, a Sham. *Counterfeit Gemms or Jewels*, Bristol-stones. Counterfeits, for the most part exceed the Truth. Thus a Flatterer pleases more than a Friend; a Braggadochio-coward thunders more than a Hero; a Mountebank promises more than a Doctor; and a Hypocrite over-acts a Religious Man, as a Counterfeit Gem is often fairer than a True one.

Country-put, a silly Country-Fellow.

Couped-up, Imprison'd, Environ'd, Surrounded, Pent up.

Court-promises, fair Speeches, or empty Promises without performances. Much the same with Court-holy-water. *Court-card*, a gay fluttering Fellow. *Court-tricks*, State-Policy.

Course, or rather

Coarse, homely, ord'nary, oppos'd to fine; as *Coarse treatment*, rough or rude Dealing; *Coarse fare*, homely Food; a *Coarse Dish*, a mean one; *Coarse or Hard-Favor'd*, oppos'd to Fair or Handsom. *Of Course*, of Custom; *out of Course*, extraordinary, or out of the way; *a Horse-Course*, a Race, also the place where the Race is Run. *A Water-course*, a

Drain. *Course of Law*, the proceedings, at Law, *The Law must have its Course*, or run freely. *I'll take a Course with you*, I'll hamper ye, or stick close on your Skirts. *A Course of Physick*, an Order or set Constitution of Physick, for a continuance or course of time. *Course of the Sun, Yearly or Daily*, a Yearly or Daily Revolution, *Course of the Moon*, the Circle of a Month.

Court-holy-water, Court Promises.

Cow-hearted, fearful or Hen-hearted.

Cows-thumb, when a thing is done exactly, nicely, or to a Hair.

Cows-baby, a Calf.

Coxcomb, a Fool; *a silly Coxcomb*, a very foolish Fellow.

Crabbed, sower, churls.

Crab-lice { *Cock*, Male. / *Hen*, Female.

Vermin breeding in Moist and Hairy Parts of the Body.

Crack, c. a Whore.

Cracker, c. an Arse; also Crust.

Crackish, c. Whorish.

Cracking, Boasting, Vaporing. *Crackt-credit*, Lost, Gone, Broken. *Crackt-title*, Unsound. *Crackt-brains*, lost Wits.

Crackmans, c. Hedges.

Cramped, a weight with a string tied to one's Toe, when a Sleep, much used by School-boies, one to another; also obstructed or hampered in any Business whatever.

Crag, a Neck; also a Rock.

Cramp-rings, c. Bolts or Shackles.

Cramp-words, difficult or uncommon.

Crank, brisk, pert.

Cranksided-ship, that does not bear Sail well.

Cranked-shells or *Stones*, wrinkled or wreathed.

Crap, c. Money. *Nim the Crap*, c. to Steal the Money. *Wheedle for Crap*, c. to coakse Money out of any Body.

Crash, c. to Kill.

Crash, the Cull, c. kill the Fellow.

Crashing-cheats, c. Teeth.

Craz'd, Mad.

Crazy, infirm or distemper'd.

Creatures, Men raised by others, and their *Tools* ever after.

Creeme, to slip or slide any thing into another's Hand.

Crew, the Coxon and Rowers in the Barge, or Pinnace, are called the *Boats-crew*, in distinction from the Complement of Men on Board the Ship, who are term'd the *Ships-company*, not *Crew*; also an ill Knot or Gang, as a *Crew of Rogues*.

Crimp, one that undertakes for, or agrees to unlade a whole Ship of Coals. *To play Crimp*, to lay or bet on one side, and (by foul play) to let t'other win, having a share of it. *Run a Crimp*, to run a Race or Horse-match fouly or knavishly. *He Crimps it*, he plays booty. *A Crimping Fellow*, a sneaking Cur.

Crinkums, the French Pox.

Crispin, a Shoe-maker, from the St. of that Name, their Patron.

Crispin's Holy-day, ev'ry Munday in the Year, but more particularly the Twenty fifth of *October*, whereon the whole Fraternity fail not to lay they Hearts in Soak.

Crochets in the crown, whimsies, Maggots.

Crockers, Forestallers, Regraters, see *Badgers*.

Croker, c. a Groat or Four-pence. *The Cull tipt me a Croker*, c. the Fellow gave me a Groat.

Crony, a Camerade or intimate Friend; *an old Crony*, one of long standing; used also for a tough old Hen.

Crop, one with very short Hair; also a Horse whose Ears are Cut.

Crop-ear'd-fellow, whose Hair is so short it won't hide his Ears.

Croppin-ken, c. a Privy, or Bog-house.

Crop-sick, Stomack-sick.

Crossbite, c. to draw in a Friend, yet snack with the Sharper.

Crosspatch, a peevish froward Person.

Crotiles, Hares Excrements.

Crow-over, to insult or domineer. *To pluck a Crow with one*, to have a bout with him. *Strut like a Crow in a Gutter*, said in jeer of the Stalking of a proud Fellow. *The Crow thinks her own Bird the Fairest*, applied to those that dote on their foul Issues. *As good Land as any the Crow Flies over*, with regard it may be, to the Crow's being a long Liver; as *no Carrion will kill a Crow*, to his being so hardy a Bird.

Crowder, a Fidler.

Crown, the top of the Head or Hat; Imperial or Regal Crown. *Where the Earth is raised* it is said, to be Crown'd with Hills, in Poetry. *The End Crowns all*, said both of the Event of Actions, and Finishing of Works. *In the Crown-Office*, Drunk; also *to Crown*, to pour on the Head.

Cruisers, c. Beggers; also nimble Friggats Coasting to and fro for Prizes, and to carry Orders, *&c.*

Crump, c. one that helps Sollicitors to *Affidavit-men*, and *Swearers*, and *Bail*, who for a small Sum will be Bound or Swear for any Body; on that occasion, putting on

good Cloaths to make a good appearance, that Bail may
be accepted.

Crump-back't, Crooked or Huncht-backt.

Crumplings, wrinkled Codlings, usually the least, but
sweetest.

Crusty-beau, one that lies with a Cover over his Face all
Night, and uses Washes, Paint, *&c.*

Cub, or *young Cub*, c. a new Gamester drawn in to be rookt;
also a young Bear, a Fox, and a Martern the first Year.

Cucumbers, Taylers.

Cucumber-time, Taylers Holiday, when they have leave to
Play, and Cucumbers are in season.

Cudgelliers, a Mob rudely arm'd; also Cudgel-Players.

Cuffin, c. a Man.

Cuffin-quire, c. see *Quire-cuffin*.

Culp, a kick, or blow; also a bit of any thing.

Culp of the Gutts, (Suffolk) a hearty kick at the Belly.

Cull, ⎰ c. a Man, a Fop, a Rogue, Fool or silly Creature
Cully, ⎱ that is easily drawn in and Cheated by Whores or
Rogues. *Cully napps us*, c. the Person Robb'd,
apprehends us. *A Bob-cull*, c. a sweet-humour'd Man to
a Whore, and who is very Complaisant. *A Curst-cull*, c.
an ill-natur'd Fellow, a Churl to a Woman.

Culm, the small or dust of Sea-coal.

Cunning-shaver, a sharp fellow.

Cup-shot, Drunk.

Cup of Comfort, as

Cup of the Creature, Strong-liquor. *A Cup too low*, when any
of the Company are mute or pensive. *To carry one's cup
even between two Parties*, to be equal and indifferent,
between them. *Many things fall out between the Cup and*

the Lip, or many things intervene between the forming
and accomplishing a Design.

Cur, a Dog of a mungrel Breed, good for nothing.

Curle, c. Clippings of Money.

Currish-fellow, snapping, snarling.

Curmudgeon, an old Covetous Fellow, a Miser.

Currant-coyn, good and Lawful Money. *Currant Custom*, a
received custom, the

Current, Stream; also humor or bent of the People.

Cursitors, c. Vagabonds; the first (old) Rank of Canters.

Curst, *a curst Cur*, a sower, surly, snarling, fierce Dog; a
Curst Cow has short Horns.

Curtals, c. the Eleventh Rank of the Canting Crew.

Curtail'd, cut off, shorten'd.

Curtezan, a gentile fine Miss or Quality Whore.

Curtain-Lecture, Womens impertinent Scolding at their
Husbands.

Cushion, *beside the Cushion*, beside the Mark.

Cut, Drunk. *Deep Cut*, very Drunk. *Cut in the Leg or Back*,
very drunk. *To Cut* c. to speak. *To Cut bene*, c. to Speak
gently, civilly or kindly; to *Cut bene* (or *bennar*) *Whidds*,
c. to give good Words. *To Cut quire whidds*, c. to give ill
Language. *A Cut* or *Chop* of Meat. *Cut and come again*, of
Meat that cries come Eat me. *A cutting wind*, very
sharp. *Of the precize Cut or Stamp*, a demure starcht
Fellow. *No Present to be made of Knives because they Cut
kindness. Ready Cut and Dried*, or turned for the purpose.
Not Cut out for it, nor turned for it. *To Cut another out of
any business*, to out-doe him far away, or excell, or
circumvent. *I'll cut you out business*, I'll find you Work
enough. A Book with Cuts or Figures; Brass or Wooden

Cutts or Prints from Copper-plates, or Wood. *A Cut throat House or Town*, where sharp and Large Reckonings are imposed, as at *Gravesend*, *Deal*, *Dover*, *Portsmouth*, *Plimouth*, *Harwich*, *Helvoetsluyce*, the *Briel*, and indeed all *Sea-ports*, nay and *Common-wealths* too, according to the observation of a late Learned Traveller in his ingenious Letters publish'd in *Holland*.

D

Dab, c. expert exquisite in Roguery. a *Rum-dab*, c. a very Dextrous fellow at fileing, thieving, Cheating, Sharping, *&c. He is a Dab at it*, He is well vers'd in it.

Dablers, in Poetry, meer Pretenders.

Dace, c. Two-pence, *Tip me a Dace*, c. Lend Two-pence, or pay so much for me.

Dag, a Gun.

Draggle-tail, a nasty, dirty Slut.

Damask the Claret, Put a roasted Orange slasht smoking hot in it.

Damber, c. a Rascal.

Damme-boy, a roaring mad, blusttring fellow, a Scourer of the Streets.

Dancers, c. Stairs.

Dandyprat, a little puny Fellow.

Dangle, to hang.

Dapper-fellow, a short, pert, brisk, tidy Fellow.

Darby, c. ready Money.

Darbies, c. Irons, Shackles or Fetters.

Darkmans, c. The night. *The Child of darkness*, c. a Bell-man.

Darkmans-Budge, c. a House-creeper, one that slides into a House in the dusk, to let in more Rogues to rob.

Dash, a Tavern-Drawer. *A Dash of Gentian, Wormwood, or stale Beer*, a slight touch or tincture of each, *to dash or brew*, as Vintners jumble their Wines together, when they sophisticate them. *A dash of Rain*, a sudden, short, impetuous pouring down, to distinguish it from a soft Shower, or a sprinkling of Rain.

Dastard, a Coward.

Dawn, Day-break or peep of Day, as the Dusk is twilight or shadow of the Evening. *One may see day at a little hole, or discover the Lyon by his Paw.*

Dawbing, bribing; also ill painting or thick laying on of Colours: Hence *bedawb'd with Gold or Silver-Lace*, when it is laid thick or close on.

Dead Cargo, not a quarter or half freighted. *To wait for dead mens shoes*, for what is little worth, or may never come to pass. *To play or work for a dead horse*, for a trifle.

Dead-men, empty-Pots or bottles on a Tarvern-table.

Dear Joies, Irishmen.

Debauchee, a Rake-hel.

Decayed Gentleman or Tradesman, broken.

Deckt-out, tricked up in fine Cloaths.

Decus, c. a Crown or five shilling-piece. *The Cull tipt me a score of Decuses*, c. my Camerade lent me five Pounds.

Deft-Fellow, a tidy, neat, little Man.

Defunct, dead and gone.

Degen, c. a Sword. *Nimm the Degen*, c. steal the Sword, or whip it from the Gentleman's Side.

Deists, against the Trinity.

Dells, c. the twenty sixth order of the canting Tribe; young bucksome Wenches, ripe and prone to Venery, but have

not lost their Virginity, which the *upright man* pretends
to, and seizes: Then she is free for any off the Fraternity;
also a common Strumpet.

Dequarting, throwing of the left Foot and Body backwards.

Dergin, a very short Man or Woman.

Desperate Fellow, fit for any lew'd Prank or Villany, *desperate
condition*, without any hopes.

Devil-drawer, a sorry Painter.

Deuseavile, c. the Country.

Deuseavile-Stampers, c. Country-Carriers.

Dews-wins, c. two Pence.

Dewitted, cut in pieces, as that great Statesman *John de
Witt*, was in Holland Anno 1672 by the Mob.

Diamond cut Diamond, bite the Biter.

Dibble, a poaking Stick to set Beans with.

Die like a Dog, to be hang'd, the worst Employment a Man
can be put to. *Die on a Fish-day, or in his shoes* the same,
die like a Rat, To be poysoned.

Dig the Badger, dislodg him.

Dimber, c. pretty.

Dimber-cove, a pretty Fellow.

Dim-mort, c. a pretty Wench.

Dimber-Damber, c. a Top-man or Prince among the Canting
Crew; also the chief Rogue of the Gang, or the
compleatest Cheat.

Dimple, a small graceful dent in the Chin called in
Ignoramus, Love's pretty Dimple.

Din, c. *what a din you keep!* what a noise you make!

Dine with Duke Humphrey, to go without a Dinner.

Ding, c. to knock down. *Ding the Cull*, c. knock down the
Fellow.

Ding-boy, c. a Rogue, a Hector, a Bully, Sharper.

Ding-dong, helter-skelter.

Dint, edge or force, *dint of the sword*, edge of the Sword, *dint of argument*, force or power of Argument.

Dippers, Ana-baptists.

Dipt, engag'd or in debt, Land pawn'd or mortgag'd. *Damnably dipt*, deep in debt, *He has dipt his Terra firma*, he has mortgaged his dirty Acres. *He has dipt his Bill*, he is almost drunk. *The cull has dipt his Tol*, c. the Spark has pawn'd his Sword. *The Dell has dipt her Rigging*, c. the Whore has pawn'd her Cloaths.

Dirty Acres, an Estate in Land.

Dirty Beau, a slovenly Fellow, yet pretending to Beauishness.

Dirty puzzle, a sorry Slattern or Slut.

Disaffection, a disorder of any part of the Body. *Disaffected to the State*. Malecontents or factious.

Disgruntled, disobliged or distasted.

Disingenuous, or indirect dealing, oppos'd to dealing on the Square.

Disguis'd, drunkish.

Dismal ditty, a Psalm at the Gallows; also a dull Ballad, or silly Song.

Dive, c. to pick a Pocket.

Diver, c. a Pick-pocket.

Doash, c. a cloak.

Dock, c. to lie with a Woman. *The Cull Dockt the Dell in the Darkmans*, the Rogue lay with a Wench all night.

Doctor, c. a false Die, that will run but two or three Chances. *They put the Doctor upon him*, c. they cheated him with false Dice.

Dog'd, followed close, way-laid. *Agree like Dog and Cat*, of those that are at variance. *Every Dog will have his day*, none so wretched but has his good Planet. A*n easy thing to find a Stick to beat a Dog*, or it costs little to trouble those that cannot help themselves. *It is an ill Dog is not worth the whistling after*; or spare to speak spare to speed. *He play'd me a Dog-trick*, he did basely and dirtily by me.

Dogged, Sullen, pouting, or in the Dumps.

Doggrel, a Term for the meanest and basest Verse; such as Ballads, *Bellmens-songs*, and the like *Meeter* of *snow hill*.

Doit, half a Farthing. Dutch Money, eight to a Penny, *not a doit left*, he has spent all.

Doll, a wooden Block to make up Commodes upon, also a Child's Baby.

Doltish, c. Foolish.

Dolthead, a Fool.

Domerars, c. Rogues, pretending to have had their Toungs cut out, or to be born dumb and deaf, who artificially turning the tip of their Toungs, into their Throat, and with a stick makeing it bleed, weak people think it the stump of their Tongue; one of whom being askt hastily *how long he had been dumb?* answer'd *but three weeks*, this is the twenty first Order of Canters, the Word also signifing Mad-men.

Dotard, An old drowsy Fellow come to Dotage.

Doudy, An ugly coarse hard favored Woman. *She is a meer Doudy*, that is, very ugly.

Dover-court, all Speakers and no Hearers.

Down-hills, c. Dice that run low.

Doxies, c. She-beggers, Trulls, Wenches, Whores, the twenty fifth Rank of *Canters*; being neither, Maids,

Wives, nor Widows, will for good Victuals, or a very
small piece of money prostitute their Bodies, protesting
they never did so before, and that meer necessity then
oblig'd them to it (tho' common Hackneys) These are
very dextrous at picking Pockets (in the action) and so
barbarous as often to murder the Children thus got.

Drab, a Whore, or Slut, a *Dirty drab*, a very nasty Slut.

Drag, a Fox's Tail.

Dragg'd, through the Horse-pond or *Bog-house*. Bailives and
Sergeants are served so that presume to arrest any
Body within the Verge of the Court-royal, or Precincts of
the Inns of Court.

Dragg'd up, as the *Rakes* call it, educated or brought up.

Dray, of Squirrels.

Drawers, c. Stockings.

Drawing, Beating the Bushes after the Fox.

Draw-Latches, c. the fourth (old) Order of the Canting
Tribe of Rogues.

Drawling in Speech, or *dreaming of Speech* when the Words are
drawn out at length, and keep as great a distance from
one another, as if they were not all of a Company.

Dreaming Fellow, a dull, drowsy, heavy Creature.

Drift, Design, Aim, Intent.

Drill, to draw in, and entice by degrees; also boring of
Pearl.

Dripper, a sort of Clap, or venereal gleating.

Dripping-weather, the same with dropping.

Dromedary, c. a Thief or Rogue, also a kind of Camel with
two bunches on his Back. *You are a purple Dromedary*, c.
you are a Bungler or a dull Fellow at thieving.

Drommerars, c. see *Domerars*.

Droppers, c. Sweetners.

Drop a cog, c. to let fall (with design to draw in and cheat) a Piece of Gold; also the piece it self.

Drop-in-his-eye, almost drunk.

Droop, to fall away, to pine, to break with Age or Infirmity, *a drooping bird* that hangs the Wing.

Drovers, Horse-leaders in Fairs, or Market, and Graziers or Drivers of Beasts.

Drub, beat with a stick or Cable-end.

Drudge, or rather *dredge*, the way of catching Oysters; also a laborious Person.

Drumbelo, a dull heavy Fellow. *A meer Drumbelo*, a very Slug.

Drunk with a continuando, de die in diem.

Dry blows, or *dry-basting* for Rib-roasting.

Dry-bob, a smart or sharp Repartee.

Dry-boots, a sly, close cunning Fellow.

Dry-drinking, without a bit of Victuals. *Dry-wine*, a little rough upon, but very grateful to the Palate.

Dry youth, sharp, close, witty.

Dub, c. a Pick-lock-key.

Dub, *the Giger*, c. open the Door. *We'll strike it upon the dub*, c. we will rob that Place.

Dubber, c. a Picker of Locks.

Dub'd, Knighted.

A Duce, c. two Pence.

Duck-leggs, short-leggs.

Dudds, c. Cloaths or Goods. *Rum dudds*, c. fine or rich cloaths or Goods.

Dudd, Cheats wonne, c. Cloaths and things stolen. *Abram Cove has wonne (or bit) Rum dudds*, c. the poor Fellow has stolen very costly Cloaths.

Dudgeon, Anger, Quarrel, Displeasure.

Duke of Exeter's Daughter, a Rack in the Tower of London, to torture and force Confession; supposed to be introduced by him, sometimes (formerly) now not in use.

Dullard, a heavy dull stupid Fellow.

Dulpickle, the same.

Dum-found, to beat soundly. *I dumfounded the sawcy Rascal.* I bang'd his Back tightly. *In the dumps*, troubled, chagrin, melancholic.

Dunaker, c. a Cow-stealer.

Duncarring, Buggering.

Dunner, a Sollicitor for Debts.

Dunn'd, teiz'd, or much importun'd.

Dunder-head, a dull heavy Creature.

Dundering Rake, a thundering Rake, or of the first Rank, one develishly lewd.

Dup, c. to enter, or open the door, *dup the ken*, c. enter the House, *dup the boozing ken and booz a gage*, c. go into the Ale-house and drink a Pot.

Durance, a Prison.

Durk, a short Dagger, in use with the *Scots*, as Stilletto is with the *Italians*.

Dusk, or Twilight, the shadow of the Evening, as Dawn is Daybreak or peep of Day.

Dust, money, *down with your Dust*, deposit your Money, pay your Reckoning. Also in another sence, *dust it away* drink quick about.

Dutchified, in the Dutch Interest, or of that Fashion.

Dutch-Reckoning, or *Alte-mall*, a verbal or Lump-account without particulars.

E

Eager, warm, or earnest in Debate; also sharp Liquors, as hard Beer, Wine turned soure, *&c.* Hence the Compounds, Vinegar, Alegar.

Eagle, c. the winning Gamester.

Earnest, c. Part or Share. *Tip me my earnest*, c. give me my Snack or Dividend.

Easy, facil, supple, pliable, managable. *He is an easy fellow*, very silly or soft, *an easy mort*, c. a forward or coming wench.

Ebb-water, c. when there's but little Money in the Pocket.

Edge-tools, as Scythes, Swords, and such as are set or ground, as Razors, Knives, Scissors, Sheers, *&c.* to distinguish them from flat Tools and Tongs, *&c.* *'tis ill jesting with Edge-tools* or trusting unexpert Men with dangerous things. *Fall back fall edge* or come what will.

Effort, an Endeavour or Proffer, *a Weak Effort*, an Offer in vain.

Egge one on, to prick him on, to provoke or stir him up. *He'll be glad to take Eggs for his money*, or to compound the matter with Loss. *You come in with your five Eggs a penny, and four of 'em addle*, of a Pragmatical Prater, or Busi-body, that wasts many Words to little purpose. *To have a Nest-egg*, to have alwaies a Reserve to come again. *As sure as Eggs be Eggs*. When nothing is so sure. *As full of Roguery as an Egg is full, of Meat.*

Elbow-grease, a derisory Term for Sweat. *It will cost nothing but a little Elbow-grease*; in a jeer to one that is lazy, and thinks much of his Labour. *Who is at your Elbow?* a Caution to a Lyer. *He lives by shaking of the Elbow*; a Gamester.

Elonge, to stretch forward the right Arm and Leg, and to keep a close Left-foot.

Elevated, pufft up; also raised to Honour, Dignity, *&c. Above the common Elevation*, above the common Level.

Eminence, a Rising opposed to a flat Ground, *rais'd to an Eminence of pitch of greatness*; to make a figure, or be a Man of mark in the World, i.e. to be conspicuous, as a City set on a Hill cannot be hid. *His Eminence*, the Title given to a Cardinal.

Empty-fellow, Silly.

Empty-skull'd, Foolish.

Empty-talk, silly, idle vain Discourse, more Noise then Sense.

Ends, Aim, Design, Drift, and variously used in composition, as, *Candle-ends, Ends of gold and silver*, Shreds of either. *Cable-ends, finger-ends* for extremity or utmost part of either. *Tis good to make both Ends meet*, or to cut your Coat according to your Cloth. Every thing has an End, and a Pudding has two.

English-cane, an oaken Plant.

English Manufacture, Ale, Beer, or Syder.

Ensnaring Questions, Interrogatories laid to trap and catch one.

Entries, where the Deer have lately passed the thickets.

Epicure-an, one that indulges himself, nice of Palate, very curious and a critick in eating.

Equip, c. to furnish one.

Equipt, c. rich; also having new Clothes. *Well equipt*, c. plump in the Pocket, or very full of Money; also very well drest. *The Cull equipt me with a brace of Meggs*, c. the Gentleman furnish'd me with a couple of Guineas.

Eriffs, Canary-birds two years old.

Evasion, a Shift, sly or indirect Answer.

Eves-drop, to be an

Eves-dropper, one that skulks, lurks at or lies under his Neighbor's Window or Door.

Ewe, or *the White Ewe*, c. a Top-woman among the Canting Crew, very Beautiful.

Execution-day, Washing-day; also that on which the Malefactors Die.

Exigence, a special or extraordinary occasion, a pinch.

Expedient, a ready shift or trick to deliver one from any difficulty, or danger near at hand.

Ey, of Pheasants, the whole Brood of young ones.

Eye-sore, an Annoyance, whatever is grievous or offensive, an unwelcome dish or guest. *All that you get you may put in your Eye and see ne'er the worse*, a pleasant Periphrasis or Round of Words, for getting nothing at all. *'Tis good to have an Eye to the main Chance*, or look to your Hits. *What the Eye ne'er sees the Heart ne'er rues*: Or out of Sight, out of Mind.

F

Facer, c. a Bumper without Lip-room.

Face in Wine, the Colour. *A good Face*, a very fine bright
Colour. *To make a Face*, to make a show or feign; also to
wryth contract or distort the Face in Contempt or
Derision. *To set a good Face upon a bad Cause*, *or Matter*,
to make the best of it. *A good Face needs no Band*, or no
advantage to set it off. *The Broad-fac'd Bird*, *or the Bird
that is all Face under Feathers*, a Periphrasis for an Owl.
Face about to the Right or Left, turn about. *to Face Danger*,
to meet it. *Facing of the Sleeve*, the Turn-up.

Facetious, full of Merry Tales and Jests, pleasantly merry.

Factitious, bodies made by Art, as Glass, Paper, and all
Compound or made Metals, as Brass, Steel, Pewter,
Latin, *&c.*

Fadge, it won't fadge or doe.

Fag, c. to Beat.

Fag'd, c. Beaten.

Fag the Bloss, c. bang the Wench.

Fag the Fen, c. drub the Whore.

Faggot the Culls, c. Bind the Men.

Faggots, Men Muster'd for Souldiers, not yet Listed.

Fair Roe-Buck, the Fifth Year.

Fair Speech, or fine Words. *Fair-spoken*, or Courteous. *A Fair Day*, or Fair Weather. *Fair in the Cradle, and foul in the Saddle*, a pretty Boy, and a hard-favor'd Man. *Soft and Fair goes far*; or not more Haste than good Speed. *Fair and far off*; wide of the Mark. *You have made a Fair Speech*, said in derision of one that spends many Words to little purpose. *A Fair or Market for Beasts. A Day after the Fair*, a Day too late, of one that has out-stayed his Markets.

Fall-a-bord, fall on and Eat heartily.

Fallacies, Cheats, Tricks, Deceipts.

Falter, to fail or more particularly a failure, or Trip of the Tongue, entangled with the Palsy, produced also from excess of Drink, or Guilt.

Famms, c. Hands.

Fambles, c. Hands.

Famble-cheats, c. Gold-rings, or Gloves.

Famgrasp, c. to agree or make up a Difference. *Famgrasp the Cove*, c. to agree with the Adversary.

Family of Love, Lewd Women, Whores; also a Sect.

Fangs, Beast-claws as talons are of a Bird.

Fanning, or refreshing of the Trees or Woods with Wind. *Fanning* or refreshing of a Close Room, opening the Windows. *Fire-fanns*, little Hand-Skreens for the Fire.

Fantastick, Whimsical, Freakish, or Capricious. *A Fantastick Dress*, very particular, remarkable.

Fardel, a Bundle.

Fardy, for Ferdinando.

Fare, Hire; also a litter of Piggs.

Farting-crackers, c. Breeches.

Fast-friends, sure or trusty.

Fastner, c. a Warrant.

Fastnesses, Boggs.

Fat, the last landed, inned or stow'd of any sort of Merchandize whatever, so called by the several Gangs of Water-side-Porters, *&c.*

Fat Cull, c. a rich Fellow. *All the Fat is in the Fire*, of a miscarriage or shrewd Turn. *Change of Pasture makes Fat Calves*, of him that thrives upon mending his Commons.

Faulkner, c. see Tumbler, first Part.

Faytors, c. the Second (old) Rank of the Canting Crew.

Feat, strange, odd.

Feats of Activity, exercise, or Agility of Body in Tumbling, turning through a Hoop, Running, Leaping, Vaulting, Wrestling, Pitching of the Bar, Quoiting, *&c.* or Slights of Hand, Tricks, Legerdemain, *&c.*

Feats of Chivalry, Exploits of War, Riding the great Horse, Tilting, Tournaments, Running at the Ring, *&c.*

Feather-bed-lane, any bad Road, but particularly that betwixt *Dunchurch* and *Daintrie*. *He has a Feather in his Cap*, a Periphrasis for a Fool. *Play with a Feather*, of things that are gamesom and full of Play, as Kittens and Kids. *To Feather his Nest*, to enrich himself by indirect means, or at the Expence of others. *Fine Feathers make fine Birds*, Gay Cloaths make fine Folks.

Feble, the narrowest Part of the Sword-blade nearest the Point.

Feinting, or Falsifying, to deceive the Adversary, by pretending to thrust in one Place, and really doing it in another.

Fence, c. to Spend or Lay out. *Fence his Hog*, c. to Spend his Shilling. *A Fence*, c. a Receiver and Securer of Stolen-goods.

Fencing Cully, a Broker, or Receiver of Stolen-goods.

Fencing-ken, c. the Magazine, or Ware-house, where Stolen-goods are secured.

Ferme, c. a Hole.

Fermerly Beggers, c. all those that have not the Sham-sores or *Cleymes*.

Ferret, c. a Tradesman that sells Goods to young Unthrifts, upon Trust at excessive Rates.

Ferreted, c. Cheated; also driven out of Holes and lurking Places, and hunted as Conies, by a little, Fierce, red-eyed Beast. Hence *Ferret-eyed*, or Eyes as red as a Ferret.

Fetch, a Trick or Wheedle. *A meer Fetch*, that is far fetched, or brought in by Head and Shoulders.

Fetids, Vegetables, or Animals, rank and strong-scented; as Garlick, Assa fœtida, *&c.* Pole-cats, Foxes, Goats, *&c.*

Fewmets, Deers excrements.

Fib, c. to beat; also a little Lie. *Fib the Cove's quarrons in the Rum-pad, for the Lour in his Bung*, c. Beat the Man in the High-way lustily for the Money in his Purse.

Fickle, mutable, or changeable, of many Minds, in a short time.

Fiddle, c. a Writ to Arrest.

Fiddle-faddle, meer silly Stuff, or Nonsense; Idle, Vain Discourse.

Fiddlers-pay, Thanks and Wine.

Filch, c. to Steal.

Filchers, c. Thieves, Robbers. *A good Filch*, c. a Staff, of Ash or Hazel, with a Hole through, and a Spike at the bottom, to pluck Cloathes from a Hedge or any thing out of a Casement.

Filching-cove, c. a Man-thief.

Filching-mort, c. a Woman-thief.

File, c. to Rob, or Cheat. *The File*, c. a Pick-pocket.

Fine-mouth'd, nice, dainty.

Finical, spruce, neat.

Finify, to trick up or dress sprucely.

Fire-drakes, Men with a Phenix for their Badge, in Livery, and Pay from the *Insurance-Office*, to extinguish Fires, covering their Heads with an Iron-pot, or Head-piece; also a Fiery Meteor, being a great unequal Exhalation inflamed between a Hot and a Cold Cloud.

Fire-ship, a Pockey Whore.

Fire-side, a Health to the Wife and Children.

Firkin of foul Stuff, a very Homely coarse corpulent Woman.

Fishing Bill, in Chancery, to make what Discoveries may be. *Who Cries Stinking Fish?* or who dispraises his own Ware? *Good Fish when it is Caught*, of what is not got so soon as reckoned upon. *All is Fish that comes to Net*, of him that flies boldly at all Game. *I have other Fish to Fry*, I am otherwise taken up, engag'd, or have other Business on my Hands.

Fixen, a froward, peevish, Child; also a She-Fox.

Fizzle, a little or low-sounding Fart.

Flabby, flimsy, not sound, firm or solid.

Flagg, c. a Groat; also a coarse rough Stone us'd in Paving. *To Flagg*, to fall off, droop, decline, or fail; also to suspend or let fall a Suit or Prosecution. *The Flag of Defiance is out*, (among the Tarrs) the Fellow's Face is very Red, and he is Drunk.

Flam, a Trick, or Sham-story.

Flanderkin, a very large Fat Man or Horse; also Natives of that Country.

Flanders-fortunes, of small Substance.

Flanders-pieces, Pictures that look fair at a distance, but coarser near at Hand.

Flapdragon, a Clap or Pox.

Flare, to Shine or glare like a Comet or Beacon.

Flash, c. a Periwig. *Rum Flash*, c. a long, full, high-priz'd Wig. *Queer Flash*, c. a sorry weather-beaten Wig, not worth Stealing, fit only to put on a Pole or dress a Scare-Crow. *Flash-ken*, c. a House where Thieves use, and are connived at.

Flasque, a Bottle (or it's resemblance) of Sand, bound about with Iron, into which the melted Metal is by Coyners and others poured; also a Pottle or five Pints and half, that quantity, formerly of *Florence*, now of any Wine: A Box for Gunpowder; a Carriage for Ordinance; an Archline somewhat distant from the corner of the Chief, and swelling by degrees toward the middle of the Escutcheon.

Flat, dead Drink; also dull Poetry or Discourse.

Flavour, Scent of Fruits; as Peaches, Quinces, *&c*. Or of Wines, as Rhenish, Canary, *&c*.

Flaunting, tearing-fine. *To Flaunt it*, to Spark it, or Gallant it.

Flaw, a water-flaw and a crack in Chrystals, as well as a speck in Gemms and Stones.

Flaw'd, c. Drunk.

Flay, to flea or skinn. *He'll flay a Flint*, of a meer *Scrat* or *Miser*.

Flear, to grinn. *A Flearing Fool*, a grinning silly Fellow.

Fleece, to Rob, Plunder or Strip; also Wooll, the true
    Golden-Fleece of *England*, a clear Spring, or Flowing
    fountain of Wealth.

Fleet, swift of Wing or Foot; in flight or Course, used not
    only of Birds upon the Wing, but of winged Arrows,
    resembling them in Flight.

Flegmatic, dull, heavy. *A Flegmatic Fellow*, a drowsy insipid
    Tool, an ill Companion.

Flesh-broker, a Match-maker; also a Bawd; between whom
    but little difference, for they both (usually) take
    Money.

Flibustiers, West-Indian Pirates, or Buckaneers,
    Free-booters.

Flicker, c. a Drinking Glass. *Flicker snapt*, c. the Glass is
    broken. *Nim the Flicker*, c. Steal the Glass. *Rum Flicker*, c.
    a large Glass or Rummer. *Queer Flicker*, c. a Green or
    ordinary Glass. *To Flicker*, to grin or flout. *Flickering*,
    grinning or laughing in a Man's Face.

Flicking, c. to cut, cutting.

Flick me some Panam and Cash, c. cut me some Bread and
    Cheese.

Flick the Peeter, c. cut off the Cloak-bag or Port-manteau.

Flip, Sea Drink, of small Beer, (chiefly) and Brandy,
    sweetned and Spiced upon occasion: *A Kan of Sir.
    Clously*, is among the Tarrs, a Kan of choice Flip, with a
    Lemon squeez'd in, and the Pill hung round.

Flippant, pert and full of Prattle.

Flimsy, flabby, not firm, sound or solid.

Flocks and Herds, Flocks are of lesser Cattel, Herds are of
    Black Cattel, a Flock of Sheep or Goats, and sometimes
    of Birds, as Pidgeons; and in Imitation of the

Gregarious Creatures, Men, that are sociable, are said to follow and flock after one another as Sheep, or to flock together to see Shows and Spectacles.

Flog, c. to Whip, *Flogg'd*, c. severely Lasht.

Flogging-cove, c. the Beadle, or Whipper in Bridewell, or any such Place.

Flogging-stake, c. a Whipping-post.

Flogg'd at the Tumbler, c. Whipt at the Cart's Arse.

Flogging, c. a Naked Woman's whipping (with Rods) an Old (usually) and (sometimes) a Young Lecher. *As the Prancer drew the Queer-Cove at the cropping of the Rotan, the Rum Pads of the Rum vile, and was Flogg'd by the Rum Cove*, c. the Rogue was dragged at the Cart's tail through the chief Streets of *London*, and was soundly Whipt by the Hangman.

Florence, a Wench that is touz'd and ruffled.

Florentine, a made Dish of Minced Meats, Currans, Spice, Eggs, *&c.* Bak'd.

Flounce, to toss, *to fling and flounce*, to fling and toss.

Flout, a jeer, to flout or jeer.

Flummery, a cleansing Dish made of Oatmeal boyl'd in Water to a kind of Jelly or Consistence and strained.

Flush in the Pocket, c. full of Money. *The Cull is flush in the Fob*, the Spark's Pocket is well Lined with Money. *Flushing in the Face*, a frequent redning, occasion'd by a sudden Question, surprize, and also from a distemper'd Liver.

Flustered. Drunk.

Flute, c. the Recorder, of *London*, or of any other Town.

Flutter, or Flie low, anciently to *Flitter*, hence a Flitter-mouse or Bat; as much as to say, a Flying Mouse, as an Owl is a Flying-Cat.

Flyers, c. Shoes.

Flying-Camps, Beggers plying in Bodies at Funerals.

Fob, c. a cheat, trick; also a little Pocket.

Fob off, slyly to cheat or deceive.

Fogus, c. Tobacco. *Tip me gage of Fogus*, c. give me a Pipe of Tobacco.

Foiling, the Footing of Deer on the Grass, scarce seen.

Folks, the Servants, or ordinary People, as Country-folks, Harvest-Folks, Work-folks, *&c. The Folks Bread or Pudding*, for the coarsest Bread or Pudding.

Fool's Coat, or *Colours*, a Motley of incongruous Colours too near a Kin to match, as Red and Yellow, which is the Fool's Coat with us, as Blew and Green is with the French. *A Fool's-Coat*, a Tulip so called, striped with Red and Yellow.

Fools-Cap, a sort of Paper so called.

Footman's Mawnd, c. an artificial Sore made with unslack'd Lime, Soap and the Rust of old Iron, on the Back of a Begger's hand, as if hurt by the bite or kick of a Horse.

Foot-pad, c. see *Low-pad*, for *one foot in the Grave*, a Pariphrasis an old Man. *He has the length of his Foot*.

Fop, Foppish, one that is singular or affected in Dress, Gestures, *&c.*

Foplin, the same, only younger.

Forebode, to presage, betoken or fore-show.

Foreboding-signs, tokens, Presages of ill Luck; as *spilling of the Salt; a Hare's crossing the Way; Croaking of Ravens; Screaking of Screach-Owls*. Or of ill Weather, either natural Signs or artificial; as, Aches, Corns, Cry of a Peacock, Water-galls, Weather-Glasses, *&c.*

Forecast, contrivance or laying a design; Precaution, or the

Wisdom of Prevention, which is beyond the Wisdom of Remedy. *To Forecast*, to contrive, or digest Matters for Execution.

Foreman of the Jury, he that engrosses all the Talk to himself.

Forestall, to antedate or anticipate.

Fork, c. a Pick-pocket. *Let's fork him*, c. let us Pick that Man's Pocket, the newest and most dextrous way: It is, to thrust the Fingers, strait, stiff, open, and very quick into the Pocket, and so closing them, hook what can be held between them.

Fork is often Rakes Heir, or after a scraping Father comes a scattering Son.

Forlorn-hope, c. losing Gamesters; also in another Sense, a Party of Soldiers, *&c.* put upon the most desperate Service.

Fort, the broad Part of the sword-blade nearest to the Hilt.

Fortune, A rich Maid, or wealthy Widdow, an Heiress.

Fortune-hunters, Pursuers of such to obtain them in Marriage. *A Creature of Fortune*, one that Lives by his Wits. *A Soldier of Fortune*, the Heir of his own Right-hand as the Spaniards call him. *A Gamester of Fortune*, one that Lives by shaking his Elbow. *He has made his Fortune*; he has got a good Estate.

Fortune-Tellers, c. the Judges of Life and Death, so called by the Canting Crew: Also *Astrologers*, *Physiognomists*, *Chiromancers*, *&c.*

Founder'd { *Horse*, Lame.
{ *Ship at Sea*, that sprung a Leak and Sunk downright.

Foundling, a Child dropt in the Streets for the Parish (the most able) to keep.

Foul Jade, an ordinary coarse Woman.

Foul Wine, when it stinks; also when unfine, or Lees flying in the Glass.

Fox, the second Year; also a sharp cunning Fellow. *Fox'd*, Drunk. *He has caught a Fox*, he is very Drunk. *An old Fox*, after the second Year; also a subtil old Fellow; also an old broad Sword. *A Fox-blade*, a Sword-blade with a Fox (or some thing like it) Grav'd on it, esteem'd good Metal.

Foxkennelleth, Lodgeth.

Foy, a farewell or taking leave, usually a Parting-glass. *To Pay his Foy*, to make his Friends Merry, before he leaves them.

Foyl-cloy, c. a Pick-pocket, a Thief, a Rogue.

Foyst, c. a Cheat a Rogue; also a close strong Stink, without Noise or Report.

Fraters, c. the eighth Order of Canters, such as Beg with a Sham-patents or Briefs for Spitals, Prisons, Fires, *&c.*

Fray, an Encounter, or Disorder. *Better come at the latter end of a Feast, than the beginning of a Fray. To Fray*, to scare or frighten; also to break or crack in wearing. Hence frail, brittle or soon broke; and when Deer rub and push their Heads against Trees to get the pells of their new Horns off.

Freak, a Whim or Maggot.

Freakish, Fantastic, Whimsical, Capricious.

Freameth, see Wild Boar.

Free-booters, Lawlesst Robbers, and Plunderers; also Soldiers serving for that Privilege without Pay, and Inroaders.

Freeholder, he whose Wife goes with him to the Ale-house;

also he that has to the Value of Fourty Shillings (or more) a Year in Land.

Freeze, a thin, small hard *Cyder* much usd by Vintners and Coopers in parting their Wines, to lower the Price of them, and to advance their Gain.

French Gout, the Pox. *A blow with a French Faggot-Stick*, when the Nose is fallen by the Pox.

Frenchified, in the French Interest or Mode; also Clapt or Poxt.

Fresh-man, a Novice, in the University.

Fresh-water-seamen, that have never been on the Salt, or made any Voyage, meer Land-Men.

Fret, to fume or chafe; also Wine in fermenting is said to be upon the *Fret*.

Fricassee, any Fried Meats; but chiefly of Rabbets.

Friggat well rigg'd, a Woman well Drest and Gentile.

Frigid, a weak disabled Husband, cold, impotent.

Frippery, old Clothes.

Froe, c. for *Urowe*, (*Dutch*) a Wife, Mistress, or Whore *Brush to your Froe, (or Bloss,) and wheedle for Crap*, c. whip to your Mistress and speak her fair to give, or lend you some Money.

Frog-landers, Dutchmen.

Frolicks, lewd or merry Pranks, pleasant Rambles, and mad Vagaries.

Frummagem'd, c. choaked.

Frump, a dry Bob, or Jest.

Fuants, Excrements of all Vermin.

Fubbs, a loving, fond Word used to prety little Children and Women; also the Name of a Yacht.

Fuddle, Drink. *This is Rum fuddle*, c. this is excellent Tipple.

Fuddle-cap, a Drunkard.

Fulsom, is a Nauseous sort of Excess; as *Fulsom fat*, loathsom fat, or fat to loathing. *Fulsom flattery*, nauseous or gross Flattery laid on too thick; as Embroidery too thick Laid on is dawbing with Gold or Silver-lace.

Fumbler, an unperforming Husband, one that is insufficient, a weak Brother.

Fumblers-Hall, the Place where such are to be put for their Nonperformance.

Fun, c. a Cheat, or slippery Trick; also an Arse. *What do you fun me?* Do you think to Sharp or Trick me? *I'll Kick your Fun*, c. I'll Kick your Arse. *He put the Fun upon the Cull*, c. he sharp'd the Fellow. *I Funn d him*, c. I was too hard for him, I out-witted or rook'd him.

Fund, or *Fond*, a Bank, or Stock or Exchequer of Money, or Moneys worth; also a Bottom or Foundation. *A Staunch Fund*, a good Security.

Funk, c. Tobacco Smoak; also a strong Smell or Stink. *What a Funk here is!* What a thick Smoak of Tobacco is here! *Here's a damn'd Funk*, here's a great Stink.

Furbish-up, to Scrub-up, to Scowre, or Refresh old Armour, *&c. He is mightily Furbish'd up on a suddain*, when a Man not accustom'd to wear fine Cloaths, gets a good Suit on his Back.

Fur-men, c. Aldermen.

Fussocks, *a meer Fussocks*, a Lazy Fat-Ars'd Wench. *A Fat Fussocks*, a Fulsom, Fat, Strapping Woman.

Fustian-verse, Verse in Words of lofty Sound and humble Sense.

Fustiluggs, a Fulsom, Beastly, Nasty Woman.

G

Ged up and down, to Fidle and Fisk, to run a Gossiping.

Gadding-gossips, way-going Women, Fidging and Fisking every where. A Gad of Steel.

Gag, c. to put Iron-pinns into the Mouths of the Robbed, to hinder them Crying out.

Gage, a Pot or Pipe. *Tip me a Gage*, c. give me a Pot or Pipe, or Hand hither, the Pot, or Pipe.

Gallant, a very fine Man; also a Man of Metal, or a brave fellow; also one that Courts or keeps, or is Kept by a Mistress. *Gallant a Fan*, to break it with Design, or Purpose to have the Opportunity and Favour to Present a better.

Gambals, Christmas Gamballs, merry Frolicks or Pranks.

Game, c. Bubbles drawn in to be cheated, also at a Bawdy-house, Lewd Women. *Have ye Any Game Mother?* Have ye any Whores Mistress Baw'd; and in another Sense. *What you game me?* c. do you jeer me, or pretend to expose me, to make a May-game of me.

Gamesome, Wanton, Frolicksom, Playful.

Gan, c. a Mouth.

Ganns, c. the Lipps.

Gang, an ill Knot or Crew of Thieves, Pickpockets or
Miscreants; also a Society of Porters under a
Regulation, and to go.

Gape-seed, whatever the gazing Crowd idly stares and gapes
after; as Puppet-shows, Rope-dancers, Monsters, and
Mountebanks, any thing to feed the Eye.

Garish, gaudy, tawdry, bedawbed with Lace, or all bedeck't
with mismatcht, or staring Colours.

Garnish-money, what is customarily spent among the
Prisoners at first coming in.

Gaume, see *Paume*.

Gaunt, lank, thin, hollow.

Gears, Rigging or Accoutrements. *Head-gear*, the Linnen or
dress of the Head. *In his Gears*, ready Rigg'd or Drest.
Out of his Gears, out of Kelter, or out of sorts. *It wont
Gee*, it won't Hit, or go.

Gelt, c. Money. *There is no Gelt to be got*, c. Trading is very
Dead.

Gentian-wine, Drank for a Whet before Dinner.

Gentry-cove, c. a Gentle-man.

Gentry-cove-ken, c. a Nobleman's or Gentleman's House.

Gentry-mort, c. a Gentlewoman.

George, c. a half Crown piece. *He tipt me forty Georges for my
Earnest*, c. he paid me Five Pounds for my Share or Snack.

Gibbrish, the Canting Tongue, or Jargon.

Gig, c. a Nose; also a Woman's Privities. *Snichel the Gig*, c.
Fillip the Fellow on the Nose. *A young Gig*, a wanton
Lass.

Gigger, c. a Door. *Dub the Gigger*, c. open the Door with the
Pick-lock that we may go in and Rob the House.

Giglers, c. wanton Women. *Gigling*, Laughing loud and long.

Gill, a Quartern (of Brandy, Wine, *&c.*) also a homely
Woman. *Every Jack must have his Gill. There's not so
Ord'nary a Gill but there's as Sorry a Jack. Gill-ale*,
Physic-ale.

Gillflurt, a proud, Minks. *Gilt*, c. a Pick-lock; also a Slut or
light Housewife.

Gimcrack, a spruce Wench; also a Bauble or Toy.

Ginger-bread, Money.

Gingerly, gently, softly, easily.

Gin, a snare or nooze, to catch Birds, as a Spring is to catch
Hares.

Gingumbobs, Toies or Baubles.

Ginny, c. an Instrument to lift up a Grate, the better to
Steal what is in the Window.

Gipp, to cure or cleanse Herrings in order to Pickling.

Girds, Taunts, Quips, Gibes or Jeers. *Bitter Girds*, Biting
sharp Reflections. *Under his Girdle*, within his Power, or
at his Beck. *If you are angry you may turn the Buckle of
your Girdle be hind you*, to one Angry for a small Matter,
and whose Anger is as little valued.

Give Nature a Fillip, to Debauch a little now and then with
Women, or Wine.

Glade, Shade.

Glance of an Eye, a Cast of the Eye; *at the first Glance*, at a
Brush, or at the first Cast.

Glanders, filthy yellow Snot at (Horses) Noses, caught from
Cold.

Glare, A Glister; also the weak Light of a Comet, Candle,
or Glow-worm. *To Glare*, or blaze like a Comet, or
Candle. Hence *Glore*, as *Pottage Glore*, or Shine with Fat.

Glaive, a Bill or Sword.

Glaver, to Fawn and Flatter. *A Glavering Fellow*, a False
Flattering Fellow.

Glaze, c. the Window.

Glazier, c. one that creeps in at Casements, or unrips Glass-
windows to Filch and Steal.

Glaziers, c. Eyes. *The Cove has Rum Glaziers*, c. that Rogue
has excellent Eyes, or an Eye like a Cat.

Glee, Mirth, Pastime.

Gleam, a weak or waterish Light; hence a Glimmering or
Twinkling of a Star.

Glib, Smooth, without a Rub. *Glib-tongued*, Voluble, ready or
Nimble-tongued.

Glim, c. a Dark-Lanthorn used in Robbing Houses; also to
burn in the Hand. *As the Cull was Glimm'd, he gangs to the
Nubb*, c. if the Fellow has been Burnt in the Hand, he'll
be Hang'd now.

Glimfenders, c. Andirons. *Rum Glimfenders*, Silver Andirons.

Glimflashy, c. angry or in a Passion. *The Cull is Glimflashy*, c.
the Fellow is in a Heat.

Glimmer, c. Fire.

Glimjack, c. a Link-boy.

Glimmerer, c. the Twenty second Rank of the Canting
Tribe, begging with Sham Licences, pretending to
Losses by Fire, *&c.*

Glimstick, c. a Candlestick. *Rum Glimsticks*, c. Silver
Candlesticks. *Queer Glimsticks*, Brass, Pewter or Iron
Candlesticks.

Glow, either to Shine or be Warm, as *Glow-worm* from the
first, and *glowing of the Cheeks*, or *glowing of Fire*, with
relation to the last.

Goads, c. those that Wheedle in Chapmen for
Horse-coursers.

Goalers-Coach, a Hurdle.

Goat, a Lecher, or very Lascivious Person.

Goatish, Lecherous, Wanton, Lustful.

Gob, c. the Mouth; also a Bit or Morsel; hence *Gobbets*, now
more in use for little Bits; as *a Chop of Meat* is a good
Cut. *Gift of the Gob*, a wide, open Mouth; also a good
Songster, or Singing-master.

God's Penny, Earnest Money, to bind a Bargain.

Gold-droppers, Sweetners, Cheats, Sharpers.

Going upon the Dub, c. Breaking a House with Picklocks.

Gold-finch, c. he that has alwaies a Purse or Cod of Gold in
his Fob.

Gold-finders, Emptiers of Jakes or Houses of Office.

Good Fellow, a Pot-companion or Friend of the Bottle.

Goose, or *Goose-cap* a Fool. *Find fault with a Fat Goose*, or
without a Cause. *Go Shoe the Goose. Fie upon Pride when
Geese go Bare-legg'd. He'll be a Man among the Geese when
the Gander is gon*, or a Man before his Mother. *A Tayler's
Goose Roasted*, a Red-hot smoothing Iron, to Close the
Seams. *Hot and heavy like a Tayler's Goose*, may be applied
to a Passionate Coxcomb.

Goree, c. Money, but chiefly Gold.

Gossips, the Godfathers and Godmothers at Christnings;
also those that are noted for

Gossiping, much Idle Prating, and Tittle Tattle.

Graces, or Ornaments of Speech. *With a good Grace*, what is
Becoming, Agreeable. *With an ill Grace*, what is
Unbecoming or Disagreeable.

Grafted, made a Cuckold of.

Grannam, c. Corn.

Grannam-gold, old Hoarded Coin.

Granny, an old Woman, also a Grandmother.

Grapple, to close in Fisticuffs or Fighting, Oppos'd to Combating at Arms-end; also a fastning of Ships together in an Engagement with Grappling Irons, a kind of Anchors (or resembling them) with four Flooks and no-Stock.

Grasp, to Catch and Holdfast, or press with the close Fist.

Grating, harsh Sounds, disagreeeable, shocking and Offensive to the ear.

Great Buck, the Sixth Year.

Great Hare, the Third Year and afterwards.

Gratings, the chequer'd Work clapt on the deck of a Ship to let in the Light and Air.

Green-bag, a Lawyer.

Green-gown, a throwing of young Lasses on the Grass and Kissing them.

Green-head, a very raw Novice, or unexperienc'd Fellow.

Greshamite, a Virtuoso, or Member of the Royal Society.

Grig, c. a Farthing; also a very small Eel. *A merry Grig*, a merry Fellow. *Not a Grig did he tip me*, c. not a Farthing wou'd he give me.

Grilliade, any Broild Meats, Fish or Flesh.

Grimace, Mops and Mows, or making of Faces.

Grim, Stern, Fierce, Surly.

Grinders, c. Teeth. *The Cove has Rum Grinders*, c. the Rogue has excellent Teeth.

Gripe or *Griper*, an old Covetous Wretch; also a Banker, Money Scrivener, or Usurer.

Griping, is an Epithet commonly affixed either to the

Exactions of Oppressive Governors, or to the Extortions
of Usurers; Griping Usurers, and griping Usury being
as ordinary in English as *Usura vorax* in Latin.

Griskins, Steaks off the Rump of Beef; also Pork-bones with
some tho' not much Flesh on them, accounted very
sweet Meat Broyled.

Gropers, c. blind Men.

Grotesque, a wild sort of Painting mostly us'd for
Banquetting or Summer-houses.

Grounds, Unscented Hair Powder, made of Starch, or Rice.
see *Alabaster*.

Grownd-Sweat, a Grave.

Growse, Heath-polts.

Growneth, the Noise a Buck makes at Rutting time.

Groyne, corruptly by the Tarrs for *Coronna*, a Seaport of
Galicia in *Spain*.

Grub-street News, false, Forg'd.

Grum, the same as *Grim*, Stern or Fierce.

Grumbletonians, Malecontents, out of Humour with the
Government, for want of a Place, or having lost one.

Grumbling of the Gizzard, Murmuring, Muttering, Repining,
Resenting.

Grunter, c. a Sucking Pig.

Grunting Cheat, c. a Pig.

Grunting Peeck, c. Pork.

Guard, of old Safeguard, now shortned into Guard, either
for State, as Princes have their Guards, or for security
so Prisoners have theirs; also the Shell of a Sword, and
the best Posture of Defence.

Gugaws, Toies, Trifles.

Gull, c. a Cheat.

Gull'd, c. Cheated, Rookt, Sharpt.

Gullet, a Derisory Term for the Throat, from *Gula*.

Gull-gropers, c. a Bystander that Lends Money to the Gamesters.

Gundigutts, a fat pursy Fellow. *In the Gun*, Drunk. *As sure as a Gun*, or Cock-sure. *Out of Gun-shot*; aloof from Danger, or out of Harm's way.

Gun-powder, an old Woman.

Gust or *Gusto*, a right Relish, Savour, or true Taste of any thing. *A Delicious Gusto*, Wines, Fruits, or Meats of a curious or pleasant Taste. *A Gust of Wind*, a short sudden, furious Blast, as we say *a Dash of Rain*, for a sudden, short, impetuous Beat of Rain.

Guzzle, Drink.

Guzzling, Drinking much.

Gut-foundred, exceeding Hungry.

Gutling, Eating much. *A Gutling Fellow*, a great Eater.

Gutter-Lane, the Throat.

Gutters, the little streak in a Deer's Beam.

Gutting, { *An House*, Rifling it, Clearing it.
{ *An Oyster*, Eating it.

Gutts, a very fat, gross Person.

Gybe, c. any Writing or Pass Sealed; also Jerk or Jeer.

Gyb'd, c. Jerkt or Whipt.

Gybing, jeering.

Gypsies, a Counterfeit Brood of wandering Rogues and Wenches, herding together, and Living promiscuously, or in common, under Hedges and in Barns, Disguising themselves with Blacking their Faces and Bodies, and wearing an Antick Dress, as well as Devising a particular *Cant*, Strolling up and down, and under colour of Fortune-Telling, Palmestry, Physiognomy, and Cure of Diseases; impose allwaies upon the unthinking Vulgar, and often Steal from them, whatever is not too Hot for their Fingers, or too Heavy to carry off. *A Cunning Gypsy*, a sharp, sly Baggage, a Witty Wench. *As Tann'd as a Gypsy*, of a Gypsy-hue or colour.

Gyrle, see *Roe*.

H

Habberdasher of Nouns and Pronouns, Schoolmaster or Usher.

Hab-nab, at Aventure, Unsight, Unseen, Hit or Miss.

Hack, the Place where the Hawk's meat is laid.

Hack and Hue, to Cut in Pieces.

Hacks or *Hackneys,* hirelings. *Hackney-whores,* common Prostitutes. *Hackney-Horses* to be let to any Body. *Hackney-Scriblers,* Poor Hirelings, Mercenary Writers.

Hackum, c. a Fighting fellow, see *Captain Hackum.*

Haddums, The Spark has been at Haddums, He is Clapt, or Poxt.

Hag, an old Witch.

Hagged, Lean Witched, Half-Starved.

Hagboat, a huge Vessel for Bulk and Length, Built chiefly to fetch great Masts, &c.

Hagbut, a Hand-gun Three quarters of a Yard long.

Haggle, to run from Shop to Shop, to stand hard to save a Penny. *A Hagler,* one that Buys of the Country-Folks and Sells in the Market, and goes from Door to Door.

Halfbord, c. Six Pence.

Half a Hog, c. Six Pence.

Half Seas over, almost Drunk.

Hamlet, c. a High Constable.

Hamper'd, caught in a Nooze, entangled, or embarassed in an intricate Affair.

Handy, Dextrous.

Handy Blows, Fisty-cuffs.

Handycrafts, the Manual Arts or Mechanic Trades. *A great Two-handed Sword*, a swinging broad Sword. *A great Twohanded fellow*, a huge swinging Fellow. *Such a thing fell into his Hand*, of one that improves another's Notion, Speech, or Invention. *He will make a Hand of it*, he will make a Penny of it, or make it turn to Account. *They are Hand and Glove*, of Friends or Camerades that are Inseparable, and almost to the same purpose. *Clove and Orange, Change Hands, and change Luck* or to Play your Cards in another Hand. *The same Hand and Fair Play*, when they Play on without changing Hands. *Many Hands make light Work. You stand with your Hands in your Pockets*, to an Idle Fellow that finds nothing to do.

Hank, He has a Hank upon him, or the Ascendant over him.

Hanker after, to Long or wish much for.

Hanktelo, a silly Fellow, a meer Cods-head.

Hans-en-kelder, Jack in the Box, the Child in the Womb, or a Health to it.

Hard Drink, that is very Stale, or begining to Sower. *Hard-drinking*, excessive Soking, or toping aboundance. *Hard Bargain*, a severe one. *Hard-favor'd*, Ugly, Homely. *Hard Frost*, a Keen or Sharp one. *Hard Case*, a severe or deep Misfortune, or ill Treatment. *Hard Master* or *Dealer*, a very near one or close.

Hare, the second Year. *A great Hare*, the third Year, *Leveret*, the first Year. *To hold with the Hare and run with the Hound*, or to keep fair with both Parties at once. *Hare-lipp'd*, Notcht or turn'd up in the middle. *Hare-sleep*, with Eies a'most open. *Hared*, Hurried. *Hare Seateth* or *Formeth*, the proper term for the Place where she Setts or Lies. *A Hare Beateth or Tappeth*, makes a noise at Rutting time. *He has swallow'd a Hare*, he is very Drunk.

Harking, Whispering on one side to borrow Money.

Harman, c. a Constable.

Harmans, c. the Stocks.

Harman-beck, c. a Beadle.

Harp-upon, a business to insist on it.

Harridan, c. one that is half Whore, half Bawd.

Hart, the Sixth Year, *A Stag*, the fifth Year. *A Staggard*, the fourth. *A Brock* the third. *A Knobber*, the second. *Hind Calf*, or *Calf*, the First.

Hart Harboureth, Lodgeth.

Hart Royal, having been Hunted by a King or Queen. *Unharbour the Hart*, Dislodge him. *A Hart Belleth*, maketh a Noise at Rutting time. *A Hart goeth to Rut*, the Term for Copulation.

Hartfordshire-kindness, Drinking to the same Man again.

Harthold or *prety Hearty*, of good Courage, or pert Spirit.

Hasty, very Hot on a sudden. *The most Haste the worst speed*, *or Haste makes Waste*, of him that loses a Business by hurrying of it. *You are none of the Hastings*, of him that loses an Opportunity or a Business for want of Dispatch.

Hatchet-fac'd, Hard-favor'd, Homely. *Under the Hatches*, in Trouble, or Prison.

Haut-bois, Oaks, Beaches, Ashes, Poplars, *&c.* Also well known and pleasant Martial Music.

Havock, Waste, Spoil. *They made sad Havock*, they Destroy'd all before 'em.

Hawk, c. a Sharper.

Hawkers, Retail News-Sellers.

Hawking, going about Town and Country with Scotch-Cloth, *&c.* or News-Papers; also Spitting difficultly.

Hay, a separate Enclosure of Wood Land; within a Forrest or Park, Fenced with a Rail or Hedge, or both. *To Dance the Hay. To make Hay while the Sun Shines*, or make good use of one's Time.

Hazy Weather, when it is Thick, Misty, Foggy.

Hazle-geld, to Beat any one with a Hazle-Stick or Plant.

Heady, strong Liquors that immediately fly up into the Noddle, and so quickly make Drunk.

Headstrong, Stubborn, Ungovernable. *A Scald Head is soon Broke.*

Head-Bully of the Pass or Passage Bank, c. the Top Tilter of that Gang, throughout the whole Army, who Demands and receives Contribution from all the Pass Banks in the Camp.

Hearing Cheats, c. Ears,

Hearts-ease, c. a Twenty shilling piece; also an ordinary sort of Strong Water; and an Herb called by some the Trinity, by others, Three Faces in a Hood, Live in Idleness, Call me to you, or Pansies, an excellent Antivenerean *&c.*

Heathen Philosopher, a sorry poor tatter'd Fellow, whose Breech may be seen through his Pocket-holes.

Heave, c. to Rob.

Heave a Bough, c. to Rob a House.

Heaver, c. a Breast.

Heavy, is either gross in Quantity, or slow in Motion, because ordinarily the one is not without the other, and therefore we say, *heavy Bodies move slowly. A heavy Fellow*, a dull Blockish Slug.

Hector, a Vaporing, Swaggering Coward.

Hedge, to secure a desperate Bet, Wager or Debt. *By Hedge or by Style*, by Hook or by Crook.

Hedge-bird, a Scoundrel or sorry Fellow.

Hedge-creeper, c. a Robber of Hedges.

Hedge-grapes, very Crabbed, wholly unfit to make Wine.

Hedge-priest, a sorry Hackney, Underling Illiterate, Vagabond, see *Patrico*.

Hedge-Tavern, or *Ale-house*, a Jilting, Sharping Tavern, or Blind *Ale-house*. *It hangs in the Hedge*, of a Law-suit or any thing else Depending, Undetermined. *As common as the Hedge, or High-way*, said of a Prostitute or Strumpet.

Hell, the Place where the Taylers lay up their Cabbage, or Remnants, which are sometimes very Large.

Hell-born-babe, a Lewd, Graceless, Notorious Youth.

Hell-cat, a very Lewd Rakehelly Fellow.

Hell-driver, a Coach-man.

Hell-hound, a Profligate, Lewd Fellow.

Helter-skelter, Pell-mell.

Hempen-widdow, one whole Husband was Hang'd.

Hem, to call after one with an inarticulate Noise.

Hemuse, see *Roe*.

Hen-hearted, Cowardly, Fearful.

Hen-peckt Friggat, whose Commander and Officers are absolutely sway'd by their Wives.

Henpeckt Husband, whose Wife wears the Breeches.

Herd of Dear or Hares, a Company.

Hick, c. any Person of whom any Frey can be made, or
   Booty taken from; also a silly Country Fellow.

Hide-bound-horse, whose Skin sticks very close, and tite like
   a Pudding Bag, usually when very Fat.

Hide-bound-muse, Stiff, hard of Delivery, *Sir J. Suckling* call'd
   Ben. Johnson's so.

Higglede-piggledy, all together, as Hoggs and Piggs lie Nose
   in Arse.

High Flyers, Impudent, Forward, Loose, Light Women; also
   bold Adventurers.

High shoon, or *Clouted-shoon*, a Country Clown.

High Pad, c. a Highway Robber well Mounted and Armed.

Highjinks, a Play at Dice who Drinks.

Hightetity, a Ramp or Rude Girl.

High Tide, c. when the Pocket is full of Money.

Hind, the Plough-boy or Ploughman's Servant at Plough and
   Cart.

Hinde, the third Year; *Hearse or Brockets Sister*, the second
   Year; *Calf* the first Year.

Hip, *upon the Hip*, at an Advantage in Wrestling or Business.

Hissing, the Note of the Snake and the Goose, the
   Quenching of Metals in the Forge; also upon any dislike
   at the Play-house, and sometimes tho' seldom in the
   Courts of Judicature, upon any foul Proceedings. The
   like is don, also in other larger Assemblies.

Hob, a plain Country Fellow; or Clown, also the Back of a
   Chimney.

Hobinal, the same.

Hobbist, a Disciple, and fond Admirer of *Thomas Hobbs*, the
   fam'd Philosopher of *Malmsbury*. *Sir Posthumus Hobby*,
   one that Draws on his Breeches with a Shoeing-horn,

also a Fellow that is Nice and Whimsical in the set of his Cloaths.

Hob-nail, a Horse Shoe-nail; also a High-shoon or Country Clown.

Hobsons-choice, that or None.

Hocus-pocus, a Juggler that shews Tricks by Slight of Hand.

Hodge, a Country Clown, also Roger.

Hodmendods, Snails in their Shells.

Hodge podge, see *Hotch-potch*.

Hog, c. a Shilling; also see *Wild-Boar. You Darkman Budge, will you Fence your Hog at the next Boozing-ken*, c. do ye hear you House Creeper, will you Spend your Shilling at the next Ale-house. *A meer Hog or Hoggish Fellow*, a greedy, covetous, morose Churl. *A Hog-grubber*, a close-fisted, narrow-soul'd sneaking Fellow. *He has brought his Hoggs to a fair Market, or he has Spun a fair Thread. Great Cry and little Wooll, as the Man said, when he Shear'd his Hoggs*, Laibour in Vain which the Latines express by *Goats-wooll*, as the English by the shearing of Hoggs. *Hogg-steer*, see *Wild Boar*.

Hogen-mogen, a Dutch Man; also High and Mighty, the Sovereign States of *Holland*.

Hogo for *Haut Goust*, a strong Scent; also a high Taste or Relish in Sauce.

Hold his Nose to the Grind-stone, to Keep him Under, or Tie Him Neck and Heels in a Bargain.

Hollow-hearted, False, Base, Perfidious, Treacherous.

Holyday-bowler, a very bad Bowler, *Holyday Cloths*, the Best. *Blind Men's Holyday*, when it is Night.

Hop-merchant, a Dancing-master. *To Hop*, denotes the Progressive Motion of Reptiles on the Ground, whence

Grasshopper, and Answers to the Fluttring or low
Flight of Insects in the Air, or Else the Transits or
Leaps of a Bird from one Perch to another in a Cage, or
the Skips of a Squirrel from Tree to Tree and Bough to
Bough in the Wood.

Homine, Indian Corn. *To beat Homine*, to pound that in a
Mortar.

Honey-moon, the first Month of Marriage.

Hood, the ancient Cover for Men's Heads, (before the Age
of Bonnets and Hatts) being of Cloath Button'd under
the Chin, not unlike a Monk's Cowl. *Two Faces under one
Hood*, a Double Dealer.

Hood wink'd, Blind-folded or Bluffed.

Hoof it, or *Beat it on the Hoof*, to walk on Foot.

Hookt, over-reached, Snapt, Trickt. *Off the Hooks*, in an ill
Mood, or out of Humor. *By Hook or by Crook*, by Fair
Means or Foul.

Hookers, c. the third Rank of Canters; also Sharpers.

Hopper-arst, when the Breech sticks out.

Horn-mad, stark staring Mad because Cuckolded.

Horse-play, any rude Boisterous sort of Sport. *You must not
look a Given Horse in the Mouth, or what is freer then Gift?
One Man may better Steal a Horse than another look on. The
Master's Eye makes the Horse Fat. An ill Horse that can't
carry his own Provender. Set the Saddle on the Right Horse*,
lay the Blame where the Fault is. *The Cart before the
Horse. A short Horse is soon Curried*, a little Business is
soon Dispatched. *The Gray Mare is the better Horse*, said
of one, whose Wife wears the Breeches. *Fallen away from
a Horse-load to a Cart-load*, spoken Ironically of one
considerably improved in Flesh on a sudden.

Host, an Inn-keeper or Victualler; also an Army. *Hostess*, a
Land-lady. *To reckon without your Host*: Or count your
Chickens before they are Hatcht.

Hot, exceeding Passionate. *Hot Work*, much Mischief done,
or a great Slaughter.

Hot-cockles, a Play among Children. *It revives the Cockles of my
Heart*, said, of agreeable News, or a Cup of Comfort,
Wine or Cordial Water.

Hot Pot, Ale and Brandy boyled together.

Hot Spur, a fiery furious passionate Fellow; also early or
forward Peas.

Hotch-potch, an Oglio or Medly of several Meats in one Dish.

House of Call, the usual lodging Place of Journey-men
Tailers.

House Tailers, Upholsterers.

How, to a Deer.

Howleth, the Noise a Wolf maketh at Rutting time.

Hubbub, a Noise in the Streets made by the Rabble.

Huckster, a sharp Fellow. *Hucksters*, the Retailers of the
Market, who Sell in the Market at second Hand. *In
Huckster's Hands*, at a desperate Pass, or Condition, or in
a fair way to be Lost.

Hue, c. to Lash; also the Complexion or Colour. *Hued*, c.
Lasht or Flogg'd. *The Cove was Hued in the Naskin*, c. the
Rogue was severe-Lasht in Bridewell. *Hue and Cry*, the
Country rais'd after a Thief.

Huff, a Bullying Fellow. *Captain Huff*, any noted Bully, or
Huffing Blade. *To Huff and Ding*, to Bounce and Swagger.

Hugger-mugger, Closely or by Stealth, Under board: *To Eat
so*, that is, to Eat by one's self.

Hulver-head, a silly foolish Fellow.

Hum-cap, old, mellow and very strong Beer.

Hum and haw, to Hesitate in Speech; also to delay, or difficultly to be brought to Consent.

Hummer, a loud Lie, a Rapper.

Hum, or *Humming Liquor*, Double Ale, Stout, Pharoah.

Hummums, a Bagnio.

Humorist, a Whimsical Fantastical Fellow.

Hump-backt, Crook-backt. *Hump-shoulder'd* or Crook-shoulder'd.

Humptey-dumptey, Ale boild with Brandy.

Hunch, to justle, or thrust.

Hunks, a covetous Creature, a miserable Wretch.

Hunting, c. decoying, or drawing others into Play.

Hunteth for his Kind, see *Otter*.

Hurly-burly, Rout, Riot, Bustle, Confusion.

Hurrican, a violent Storm or Tempest; also a disorder or confusion in Business.

Hurridun, see *Harridan*.

Hush, very still, quiet. *All was Hush*, a great or profound Silence. *Husht up*, concealed, or clapt up without Noise.

Husky-lour, c. a Guinea, or Job.

Hussy, an abbreviation of Housewife, and sometimes a Term of Reproch, as, *how now Hussy*, or *she is a Light Hussy*, or Housewife.

Hut, from; a Term much us'd by Carters, *&c*. Also, a little House or slight Abode for Soldiers, Peasants, *&c*.

Huzza, Originally the Cry of the *Huzzars*, or Hungarian Horsemen; but now the Shouts and Acclamations, of any Soldiers, or of the Mob.

I J

Jabber, to Talk thick and fast, as great Praters do, or to Chatter like a Magpye.

Jack, c. a Farthing, a small Bowl (the mark) to throw at, an Instrument to draw on Boots, hence *Jack-boots*; also a Leathern Vessel to Drink out of, and an Engine to set the Spit a going. *Jack in an Office*, of one that behaves himself Imperiously in it. *Every Jack will have a Gill*, or the Coursest He, will have as Coarse a She. *He wou'dn't tip me Jack*, c. not a Farthing wou'd he give me.

Jack-adams, a Fool.

Jack-a dandy, a little impertinent insignificant Fellow.

Jack Kitch, c. the Hangman of that Name, but now all his Successors.

Jack in a Box, c. a Sharper, or Cheat.

Jackanapes, a Term of Reproach, a little sorry Whipper-snapper; also a well known waggish Beast. As full of Tricks as a *Jackanapes*.

Jack-sprat, a Dwarf, or very little Fellow, a Hop-on-my-thumb.

Jack at a Pinch, a poor Hackney Parson.

Jack-hawk, the Male.

Jacobites, Zealous Sticklers for the late King *James*, and his
    Interest; also sham or Collar Shirts, and Hereticks *Anno*
    530, following one *Jacobus Syrus*, who held but one Will,
    Nature and Operation in Christ, Circumcision of both
    Sexes, *&c.*

Jade, a Terme of Reproch given to Women, as *Idle Jade*,
    Lazy Jade, silly Jade, &c. As *dull Jade, tired Jade*, to a
    heavy or over-ridden Horse.

Jakes, a House of Office.

Jague, c. a Ditch.

Janizaries, formerly, only the Grand Signior's Foot Guard,
    chosen out of Tributary Christians, taken early from
    their Parents, and perverted to Mahumetanism, ever
    accounted their best Soldiers; but now any Prince's or
    great Man's Guards; also the Mob sometimes so called,
    and Bailives, Serjeants, Followers, Yeomen, Setters, and
    any lewd Gang depending upon others.

Jarke, c. a Seal.

Jarke-men, c. the Fourteenth Order of the Canting Tribe;
    also those who make Countefeit Licences and Passes,
    and are well paid by the other Beggers for their
    Pains.

Jarrs, Quarrels, Disputes, Contentions.

Jason's Fleece, c. a Citizen cheated of his Gold.

Jayl-birds, Prisoners.

Ice-houses, Repositories to keep Ice and Snow under
    Ground all Summer, as there are Conservatories to
    House Orange-Trees, Limes, and Myrtles in the
    Winter. *Break Ice in one place and it will Crack in more*,
    or find out one slippery Trick, and suspect another.

When the Ice is once broke, or when the Way is open
others will Follow. *Ice* or *Icicles*, little pendulous pieces
of Ice under the Eaves.

Idioms, Proprieties of any Speech or Language, Phrases or
particular Expressions, peculiar to each Language.

Idio-syncrasies, peculiar Constitutions, or Affections,
incident only in particular to some Temperaments, as
several Sympathies and Antipathies, as different and
unaccountable as the Variety of Gifts and Talents in
Men.

Jenny, c. an Instrument to lift up a Grate, and whip any
thing out of a Shop-window.

Jesses, short Strapps of Leather fastned to the Hawk's
Leggs.

Jetting along, or *out*, a Man Dancing in his Gate, or Going;
also a House starting out farther than the rest in the
Row.

Jew, any over-reaching Dealer, or hard, sharp Fellow. *He
treated me like a Jew*, he used me very barbrously.

Jews, Brokers behind St. *Clement*'s Church in *London*, so
called by (their Brethren) the Tailers.

Ignoramus, a Novice, or raw Fellow in any Profession; also,
we are Ignorant, written by the Grand Jury upon Bills,
when the Evidence is not Home, and the Party
(thereupon) Discharg'd.

Jig, a Trick; also a well known Dance. *A Pleasant Jig*, a
witty, arch Trick.

Jigget, (of Mutton) the Leg cut off with part of the Loin.

Jilt, a Tricking Whore.

Jilted, abused by such a one; also deceived or defeated in
one's Expectation, especially in Amours.

Jingling, the Noise of Carriers Horses Bells, or Ringing of Money that chinks in the Pocket.

Jingle-boxes, c. Leathern Jacks tipt and hung with Silver Bells formerly in use among Fuddle caps.

Jinglers, c. Horse-Coursers frequenting Country Fairs.

Jingle-brains, a Maggot-pated Fellow.

Jiniper-Lecture, a round scolding Bout.

Ill fortune, c. a Nine-pence.

Ill-mann'd, a Hawk not well broke, taught or train'd.

Impost-taker, c. one that stands by and Lends Money to the Gamester at a very high Interest or Premium.

Implement, Tool, a Property or Fool, easily engag'd in any, (tho' difficult or Dangerous) Enterprize.

Importunate, Dunning, pressing.

Importunity of Friends, the stale Excuse for coming out in Print, when Friends know nothing of the Matter.

Inadvertency, any slip or false step, for want of Thinking and Reflection.

Inching-in, Encroaching upon. *One of his Inches*, of his Size or Stature. *Won by Inches*, dearly or by little and little. *Give you an Inch and you'll take an Ell*, of one that presumes much on little Encouragement.

Incog, for Incognito, a Man of Character or Quality concealed or in disguise.

Incongruous, or *an Incongruity*; Treating any Person not according to his Character, or appearing in any Country, without conforming to the Habits and Customs of the Place, as teaching a General the Art of War, talking with an Ambassador without his Language, or the help of an Interpreter, moving the Hat to *Turks*, that never stirr their Turbants, or calling for a

Chair with such Nations, as sit alwaies crosse-legg'd upon Carpets.

Indecorum, any violation of the Measures of Congruity, in Story, Painting, or Poetry, as introducing Persons together that are not Contemporaries, and of the same Age, or representing them with Habits, Arms or Inventions, unknown to their Times, as the *Romans* with Gunns or Drumms, which wou'd be no less Preposterous and Absurd than Painting the Noblemen of *Venice* on Horseback, or describing the *West Indians* before the Arrival of the *Spaniards*, with the Shipping, Horses, and Arms of the *Europeans*.

Indulto, his Catholic Majesty's Permission to the Merchants to unlade the Galeons, after his Demands are adjusted.

In his Ale or *Beer*, Drunk, tho' it be by having too much of that in him.

Iniskilling-men, fam'd for their Prowess, in the late Irish Wars; also the Royal Regiment (of Citizens) in derision so called, soon rais'd, and as soon laid down.

Inke, the Neck from the Head to the Body of any Bird the Hawk doth prey upon.

Inkle, Tape. *As great as two Inkle-makers*, or as great as Cup and Cann.

Inlayed, well inlayed, at ease in his Fortune; or full of Money.

Inmates, Supernumeraries, who have no House or Being of their own, and yet are no Members of the House or Family they Live in, from whom they differ in the same Nature, as the Excrescences of Trees do from the Fruits either Genuin or Grafted; as Misletoe of the Oak, Galls, *&c.* differ from the Mast or Acorns.

Insipids, Block-heads; also things that are tastless.

Interlopers, Hangers on, retainers to, or dependers upon other folks; also Medlers and Busybodies, intruders into other Men's Professions, and those that intercept the Trade of a Company, being not legally authorized.

Intrigues, Finesses, Tricks of War, or State, as Court-tricks, Law-quirks, tho' in War they are rather called Stratagems.

Intriguing, Plotting, Tricking, Designing, full of Tricks and Subtilties.

Inveterate, either Enemies that are implacable and of long continuance, or Diseases that are confirmed, deep-rooted and riveted.

Joan, a *homely Joan*, a Coarse Ord'nary Woman, *Joan in the Dark is as good as my Lady*, or when the Candles are out all Cats art Gray.

Job, c. a Guinea, Twenty shillings, or a Piece. *Half a Job*, c. half a Guinea, Ten shillings, half a Piece, or an Angel.

Jobbers, see Badgers, Matchmakers, Salesmen, Stock-jobbers.

Jobbernoll, c. a very silly Fellow.

Jock or *Jockumcloy*, c. to copulate with a Woman.

Jockum-gage, c. a Chamberpot. *Tip me the Jockum-gage*, c. give me or hand me the Member-mug. *Rum Jockum-gage*; c. a Silver-chamberpot.

Jockey's, rank Horse-Coursers, Race Riders, also Hucksters or Sellers of Horses, very slippery Fellows to deal with.

Jolter-head, a vast large Head; also Heavy and Dull. *To Jolt or Shake*, jolting or shaking of a Coach.

Jordain, c. a great Blow or Staff; also a Chamberpot. *I'll tip him a Jordain if I transnear*, c. I will give a Blow with my Staff if I get up to him.

Joseph, c. a Cloak or Coat. *A Rum Joseph*, c. a good Cloak or
    Coat. *A Queer Joseph*, c. a coarse ord'nary Cloak or
    Coat; also an old or Tatter'd one.

Irish Toyles, c. the Twelfth Order of Canters; also Rogues
    carrying Pinns, Points, Laces, and such like Wares
    about, and under pretence of Selling them, commit
    Thefts and Robberies.

Iron-doublet, a Prison.

Itch-land, Wales.

Jugglers, Nimble and expert Fellows at Tricks, and Slights
    of Hand, to distinguish them from Tumblers, that
    perform Bodily Feats, or Feats of Activity, by playing of
    Tricks with the whole Body.

Jukrum, c. a License.

Jumble-gut-lane, any very bad or rough Road. *To Jumble*, to
    shake much or often.

Justice, I'll do Justice Child, c. I will Peach or rather Impeach
    or Discover the whole Gang, and so save my own
    Bacon; also in another Sense, *I'll do you Justice Sir*, I will
    Pledge you.

K

Kate, c. a Pick-lock. *'Tis a Rum Kate*, c. that is a Cleaver Pick-lock.

Keel-bullies, Lighter-men that carry Coals to and from the Ships, so called in Derision.

Keel-hale, to draw by a Rope tied to the Neck and fastned to a Tackle (with a jerk) quite under the Keel or bottom of the Ship.

Keffal, a Horse.

Kelter, *out of Kelter*, out of sorts.

Ken, c. a House. *A bob Ken*, or *a Bowman-ken*, c. a good or well Furnished House, full of Booty, worth Robbing; also a House that Harbours Rogues and Thievs. *Biting the Ken*, c. Robbing the House.

Ken-miller, c. a Housebreaker. *Friend John, or sweet Tom, 'tis a bob Ken, Brush upon the Sneak*, c. 'tis a good House, go in if you will but Tread softly, and mind your Business. *Now we have Bit*, c. the House is Robb'd, or the Business is done. *There's a Cull knows us, if we don't pike he'll Bone us*, c. that Fellow sees us, if we don't scour off, he will Apprehend us. *Ding him*, c. Knock him Down.

Then we'll pike, tis all Bowman, c. we will be gone, all is well, the Coast is clear.

Keeping Cully, one that Maintains a Mistress, and parts with his Money very generously to her.

Kicks, c. Breeches. *A high Kick*, the top of the Fashion; also singularity therein. *Tip us your Kicks, we'll have them as well as your Loure*, c. pull off your Breeches, for we must have them as well as your Money.

Kid, c. a Child; also the first Year of a Roe, and a young Goat.

Kidnapper, c. one that Decoys or Spirits (as it is commonly called) Children away, and Sells them for the Plantations.

Kidder, c. see *Crocker*.

Kidlay, c. one who meeting a Prentice with a Bundle or Parcel of Goods, wheedles him by fair Words, and whipping Sixpence into his Hand, to step on a short and sham Errand for him, in the mean time Runs away with the Goods.

Kidney, (Beans) French. *Of that Kidney*, of such a Stamp. *Of a strange Kidney*, of an odd or unaccountable Humor.

Kilkenny, c. an old sorry Frize-Coat.

Kill-Devil, Rum. *Kill two Birds with one Stone*, Dispatch two Businesses at one Stroak.

Kimbaw, c. to Trick, Sharp, or Cheat; also to Beat severely or to Bully. *Let's Kimbaw the Cull*, c. Let's Beat that Fellow, and get his Money (by Huffing and Bullying) from him.

Kinchin, c. a little Child.

Kinchin-coes, c. the Sixteenth Rank of the Canting Tribe, being little Children whose Parents are Dead, having been Beggers; as also young Ladds running from their Masters, who are first taught Canting, then thieving.

Kinchin-cove, c. a little Man.

Kings Head Inn, or *the Chequer Inn in Newgate-street*, c. the Prison, or Newgate.

King's Pictures, c. Money.

King of all Beasts of Venery, a Hare.

King of the Gypsies, the Captain, Chief, or Ring-leader of the Gang, the Master of Misrule.

Kindly, Fruit, or Season, towardly. *Kindness will creep where it cannot go.*

Kinchin-morts, c. the Twenty seventh and last Order of the Canting Crew, being Girls of a Year or two old, whom the *Morts* (their Mothers) carry at their Backs in *Slates* (*Sheets*) and if they have no Children of their own, they borrow or Steal them from others.

Kissing the Maid, an Engine in *Scotland*, and at *Halifax* in *England*, in which the Head of the Malefactor is Laid to be Cut off, and which this way is done to a Hair, said to be invented by Earl *Morton* who had the ill Fate to Handsel it. *Kissing goes by Favour*, I suppose another sort is meant by this Proverb than the foremention'd.

Knack, or Slight in any Art, the Craft or Mystery in any Trade, a petty Artifice, or Trick like those upon the Cards. *Knacks* or Toies, *a Knack-shop*, or Toy-shop, freight with pretty Devices to pick-Pockets.

Knave in Grain, one of the First Rate. *Knaves and Fools are the Composition of the whole World.*

Knight Errant, the Knight or Hero in Romances, that alwaies is to Beat the Giant, and Rescue the destressed Damsel.

Knight -Errantry, Romantick and Fabulous Exploits, out of
the common Road, and above the ordinary Size, such as
the wild Adventures of wandering Knights.

Knight of the Blade, c. a Hector or Bully.

Knight of the Post, c. a Mercenary common Swearer, a
Prostitute to every Cause, an Irish Evidence.

Knight of the Road, c. the chief High-wayman best Mounted
and Armed, the Stoutest Fellow among them.

Knobber, see Hart.

Knock in the Cradle, a Fool.

Knock down, very strong Ale or Beer.

Knock off, to give over Trading; also to Abandon or Quit
one's Post or Pretensions.

*Knowledge is no Burden. Knowledge makes one laugh, but wealth
makes one dance.*

Knot, a choice Bird, something less than a Ruff.

Knotting, making Fringe.

L

Labourinvain, lost Labour, such as washing of Blackamoors, shearing of Hoggs, hedging in the Cuckoe, *&c.*

Lac'd { *Coffee*, Sugar'd.
{ *Mutton*, a Woman.

Lacing, Beating, Drubbing. *I'll Lace your Coat Sirrah*, I will Beat you soundly.

Ladder, see *Badger* first Part.

Lady, a very crooked, deformed and ill shapen Woman.

Lady-birds, Light or Lewd Women; also a little Red Insect, variegated with black Spots.

Lag, c. Water; also Last.

Lag-a dudds, c. a Buck of Cloths. *As we cloy the Lagg of Dudds*, come let us Steal that Buck of Cloths. *To Lagg behind*, or come after with Salt and Spoons. *Lagg of the Flock*, the Hindmost.

Lambaste, to Beat soundly.

Lamb-pye, Beating or Drubbing.

Lamb-skin-men, c. the Judges of the several Courts.

Lambs-wool, roasted Apples and Ale.

Lame Excuse, a sorry Shift or Evasion.

Land-lopers or *Land-lubbers*, Fresh-water Seamen so called
   by the true Tarrs; also Vagabonds that Beg and Steal
   about the Country.

Land-pirates, c. Highwaymen or any other Robbers.

Land-lord and *Land-lady*, Host and Hostess; also
   Possessors of Land or Houses, and Letters out of either
   to farm or for Lodgings. *How lies the Land?* How stands
   the Reckoning? *Who has any Lands in Appleby?* a
   Question askt the Man at whose Door the Glass
   stands Long.

Lank, Gaunt, Thin, Hollow, Lean, Meager, Slender, Weak.
   Lank Ears of Corn, very thin Ears.

Lanspresado, c. he that comes into Company with but Two
   pence in his Pocket.

Lantern-jaw'd, a very lean, thin faced Fellow. *A Dark-
   Lanthorn*, the Servant or Agent that Receives the Bribe
   (at Court.)

Lap, c. Pottage, Butter-milk, or Whey. *'tis rum Lap*, c. this
   is excellent Soupe.

Larbord, on the left side or Hand.

Lare-over, said when the true Name of the thing must (in
   decency) be concealed.

Largess, a Pittance properly given to Reapers and Harvest
   Folks, now used for any petty Donative, or small
   Gratuity.

Latitudinarian, a Churchman at large, one that is no Slave
   to Rubrick, Canons, Liturgy, or Oath of Canonical
   Obedience, and in fine looks towards *Lambeth*, and
   rowes to *Geneva*.

Layd-up-in Lavender, when any Cloaths or other Moveables
   are pawn'd or dipt for present Money; also *Rodds in*

Pickle, of Revenge in reserve, till an opportunity offers to show it.

Lawn, a naked Space in the middle of a Park or Forrest, left Untilled, and without Wood, contrary to a *Hay*, which see in it's proper Place; also very thin Linnen, formerly much Worn.

Layr, the Impression where any Deer hath Harboured or reposed.

Leachers, Lascivious or Lustful Men.

Leaden Pate, a dull, heavy, stupid Fellow.

Leaders, the first Players, Generals of Armies, and Men of most sway in great Councils or Assemblies; also the Fore-horses in Coaches and Teams. *Who Leads?* Who begins or Plays first.

Leash, Three; also the String where with a Grey-hound is Led.

Leather-head, a Thick-skull'd, Heavy-headed Fellow.

Leather-Mouth'd Fish, Carp, Roach, *&c.* having their Teeth in their Throats.

Leathern Convenience, (by the Quakers) a Coach.

Leaves, of a Tree, of a Book, of Doors, or Window-shutters, and of folding Tables; *I must turn over a new Leaf with you*, or take another Course with you.

Legerdemain, Jugglers Tricks; also Sharping.

Lesses, Boars Excrements.

Lets take an Ark and Winns, c. let us hire a Skuller.

Let's buy a Brush or *Let's Lope*, c. let us scour off, and make what shift we can to secure our selves from being apprehended. *Let him Laugh that Wins: Let the World say what they will, if I find all well at Home. Let every Man meddle with his own.*

Leveret, the first Year, see *Hare.*

Levite, a Priest or Parson; also those of the Tribe of Levi, whose Inheritance the Priest-hood (craft and all) was.

Levy, the Prince's, or any great Man's time of Rising.

Leystall, a Dunghil.

Lib, c. to Tumble or Lye together.

Libben, c. a private dwelling House.

Libbege, c. a Bed.

Libkin, c. a House to Lye in; also a Lodging.

Libertines, Pleasant and profuse Livers, that Live-apace, but wildly, without Order, Rule, or Discipline, lighting the Candle (of Life) at both Ends. *A short Life and a Merry one. Life is sweet. Life is half Spent, before we know what it is.*

Lickt, Pictures new Varnished, Houses new Whitened, or Women's Faces with a Wash.

Lifter, c. a Crutch.

Light Finger'd, Thievish.

Light-mans, c. the Day or Day-break.

Light Friggat, a Whore; also a Cruiser.

Light Woman, or *Light Huswife*, Lewd, Whorish.

Light-timber'd Fellow, limber or slender Limb'd; also weak.

Lilly-white, c. a Chimney-sweeper.

Linnen-armorers, c. Tailers.

Line of the old Author, a Dram of Brandy.

Litter, any thing clatter'd up, out of Place or Order, *What a litter here is?* What a toss and tumble? Also *a Litter of Cubbs*, young Foxes; *of Whelps*, *Puppies*, young Doggs.

Little Barbary, Wapping.

Little Fellow or Action, Contemptible Base, Sneaking, Ungentleman-like.

Loblolly, any ill-cookt Mess.

Lob-cock, a heavy, dull Fellow. *In Lob's Pound*, Laid by the Heels, or clap'd up in Jail.

Lobster, a Red Coat Soldier.

Lock all fast, c. one that Buys and Conceals Stolen Goods. *The Lock*, c. the Magazine or Ware-house whither, the Thieves carry Stolen Goods to be secur'd; also an Hospital for Pockey Folks in *Kent-street*.

Lockram-jaw'd, Thin, Lean, Sharp-visag'd.

Loge, c. a Watch. I suppose from the French *Horloge*, a Clock or Watch. *Filed a Cly of a Loge, or Scout*, c. Pickt a Pocket of a Watch. *Biting a Loge, or Scout*, c. the same.

Loggerhead, a heavy, dull Fellow. *To go to Loggerheads*, to go to Fisticuffs.

Lolpoop, a Lazy, Idle Drone. *To Loll*, to Lean on the Elbows; also to put out the Tongue in derision.

Long-headed, Wise, of great reach and foresight.

Long-meg, a very tall Woman.

Long-shanks, Long-legged.

Long-winded Pay-master, one that very slowly, heavily, or late Paies.

Looby, a lazy dull Fellow.

Looking-glass, a Chamber-pot.

Loon-slatt, c. a Thirteen Pence half Penny. *A Loon*, see *Lout*. *A False Loon*, a true *Scotch* Man, or Knave of any Nation.

Lord, a very crooked deformed, or ill-shapen Person.

Lore, Learning or Skill in any Thing.

Louse-land, Scotland. *A Scotch Louse-trap*, a Comb.

Lout, an heavy, idle Fellow. *To Lout*, to Low like a Cow, or Bellow like a Bull.

Loure, c. Money.

Low Tide, When there's no Money in a Man's Pocket.

Low-pad, c. a Foot-Pad.

Lubber, Lubberly, a heavy, dull Fellow.

Lud's-bulwark, c. Ludgate Prison.

Luggage, Lumber.

Luggs, Ears: Hence to Lug by the Ears. *Ye can he make a Silk-Purse of a Sowe's Luggs*, a Scotch Proverb. *To Lug out*, to draw a Sword.

Lullaby-cheat, c. a Child,

Lumber, Rubbish, Trash, Trumpery.

Lumpish, heavy dull, drowsy.

Lurched, Beaten at any Game. *Left in the Lurch*, Pawn'd for the Reckoning, or left at Stake to Smart for any Plot.

Lure, c. an idle Pamphlet; also a Bait. *Throw out a Lure*, to lay Bait.

Lurries, c. Money, Watches, Rings, or other Moveables.

Lyome, the String wherewith a Hound is Led.

M

Mab, a Slattern. *Mab'd up*, Drest carelesly, like a Slattern, of such a one it is said, *Her Cloths sit on her, like a Saddle on a Sow's Back*. *Queen Mab*, Queen of the Fairies.

Mackarel, c. a Bawd.

Mackarel-back, a very tall, lank Person.

Machiavilian, one wickedly or knavishly Politic.

Machines, Vessels full of Carcasses and Bombs, under Shelter or Covert of the *Smokers*, to come close up under Walls, Forts, Fortifications, *&c.*, being fixt to Blow up the same. Also Engines or Instruments of divers Arts, and Movements upon the Stage.

Madam Van, c. a Whore, *The Cull has been with Madam Van*, c. the Fellow has enjoyed such a one.

Mad-cap, a frolicksom Person.

Made, c. Stolen. *I Made this Knife at a heat*, c. I Stole it cleaverly.

Mad Tom, alias of Bedlam, the Eighteenth Rank of Canters.

Madge-howlet, an Owl.

Maggot, a whimsical Fellow, full of strange Fancies and Caprichio's, *Maggotty*, Freakish.

Maiden-sessions, when none are Hang'd.

Mailes, the Breast-Feathers of a Hawk.

Main, great, excellent, choice, rare; also the Sea. *Maingood*, very good. *With Might and Main*, Tooth and Nail.

Make, c. a half Penny.

Make-bait, c. Trouble-House, or Mischief-maker, a stirrer of Strife, and maker of Debate, a Boute feu, or Incendiary.

Male-contents, Disaffected to the State, out of Humor with the Government.

Malkin or *Maukin*, Scare-crow, Drest and Set up to fright the Birds. Also a Scovel (of old Clouts) to cleanse the Oven: Hence *Malkin-trash*, for one in a rueful Dress, enough to Fright one. *There are more Maids than Malkins*, *Mawks*, the same abbreaviated. *Mawkish*, a Wallowish, ill Tast.

Malmesey-nose, a jolly, red Nose.

Man o' th' Town, a Lew'd Spark, or very Debaushe.

Manning, a Hawk, making him endure Company.

Mannikin, a Dwarf, or diminutive Fellow.

Mantles, when Drink is brisk and smiles; also when a Hawk stretcheth one of her Wings after her Leggs, and so the other.

Margery-prater, c. a Hen.

Marinated, c. Transported into some forreign Plantation; also Fish Soused.

Marriage-music, Childrens Cries.

Marks, the Footing of an Otter.

Marrel, a Bird about the bigness of a Knot, but not good Meat.

Martern, a Wild Cat, the second Year, called a Cub, the first.
　　A Martern Treeth, Lodgeth; *Tree the Martern*, Dislodge him.

Masons-mawn'd, c. a Sham sore above the Elbow, to counterfeit a broken Arm, by a Fall from a Scaffold, expos'd by subtil Beggers, to move Compassion, and get Money.

Masons-Word, who ever has it, shall never want, there being a Bank at a certain Lodge in *Scotland* for their Relief. 'Tis communicated with a strict Oath, and much Ceremony, (too tedious to insert) and if it be lent to any of the Society, he must, (nay will) come immediately, tho' very Busy, or at great Distance.

Match or *Make*, the Copulation of Woolves.

Match-makers, a better sort of Procurers of Wives for Men, or Husbands for Women, Maiden-head-jobbers, Virginity Sellers, Brokers, *&c.*

Maul'd, swingingly Drunk, or soundly Beat.

Maunders, c. Beggers.

Maund-ing, c. to Beg, Begging.

Maundring-broth, Scolding.

Mawdlin, weepingly Drunk, as we say the Tears of the Tankard. *What are you Mawdlin you Rake?* are ye' neither Drunk, nor Sober?

May-games, Frolicks, Plaies, Tricks, Pastimes *&c. Do you make a May-game of me?* do you Abuse or Expose me?

Mead, A pleasant Summer Drink, made of Water and Honey, Boyled, and Bottled fine, in great vogue in *Moscovy*, where 'tis said the best in the World is made.

Meadites, a Faction of Quakers, that follow most, and are in the Interest of *Mead*.

Meal-mouth, a sly, sheepish Dun, or Sollicitor for Money.

Measure, the Distance of Duellers. *To break Measure*, to be out of the Adversaries reach.

Mechanic, a Tradesman; also a mean, inconsiderable, contemptible Fellow.

Meggs, c. Guineas. *We fork'd the rum Cull's Meggs to the tune of Fifty*, c. We Pickt the Gentleman's Pocket of full Fourty Guineas.

Mellow, a'most Drunk; also smooth, soft Drink.

Melt, c. to spend Money. *Will you Melt a Bord?* Will you spend your Shilling? *The Cull Melted a couple of Decusses upon us*, c. the Gentleman spent ten Shillings upon us.

Member-mug, a Chamber-pot.

Mercury, Wit; also Quick-silver, and a Courant or News-Letter.

Mercurial, Witty, also one Born under ☿, *i.e.* when that Planet is Lord of the Horoscope or Ascendant at Birth.

Marcury Women, Whole-sale News-sellers, who Retail to the *Hawkers*.

Metheglin, a strong Drink, made of new Wort and Honey.

Mew, when Deer cast their Horns; also the Place where the Hawk is set down, during the time she raiseth her Feathers.

Meyny, the Folks, or Family-Servants. Hence Menial-Servant, yet in use, for a Domestic or Family-Servant.

Mifty, apt to take Pet, or be out of Humor.

Mill-clapper, a (Woman's) Tongue. *As Safe as a Thief in a Mill*, a waggish Periphrasis for a Miller, who is a Thief by his Trade.

Milch-kine, a Term us'd by Goalers, when their Prisoners will bleed freely to have some Favor, or be at large.

Mill, c. to Steal, Rob, or Kill.

Mill-a-ken, c. to Rob a House, *Milling the Gig with a Betty*, c. Breaking open the Door with an Iron-Crow. *Milling the Glaze*, c. Breaking open the Window. *Mill them*, c. Kill them.

Miller, c. a Killer or Murderer.

Mill-a-crackmans, c. to break a Hedge.

Mill-a-bleating-cheat, c. to kill a Sheep.

Mill a-grunter, c. to Kill a Pig.

Mil-ken, c. a House-breaker. *Mill the Gig with a Dub*, c. to open the Door with a Pick-lock or false Key.

Miller's-Thumb, or *Bull-head*, a Fish with a broad Head, and wide Mouth, two Finns near his Eyes, and as many under his Belly, and on his Back, and one below the Vent, his Tayl round, and his Body cover'd with Whitish, Blackish and Brownish Spotts.

Mince the Matter, to tell it Sparingly or by Halves.

Miniature, Painting in little.

Minks, a proud Flirt.

Mint, c. Gold; also a late Sanctuary (in *Sowthwark*) for such as broke either out of Necessity, or in Design to bring their Creditors the more easily to a Composition. Hence *Minters*, the Inhabitants.

Miquelets, Mountaneers, (in *Spain*) or Spanish Rapparies.

Miscreant, a lewd, wicked Fellow.

Mish, c. a Shirt or Smock.

Mish-topper, c. a Coat or Petticoat.

Miskin, a Dunghil or Lay-stall.

Miss, a Whore of Quality; also a little Girl.

Moabites, Serjeants, Bailiffs and their Crew.

Mob,
Mobile, } the Vulgar, or Rabble.
Mobility,

Mock-song, that Ridicules another Song, in the same Terms

and to the same Tune. *A Mock-Romance*, that ridicules
other Romances, as *Don Quixot*. *A Mock-Play*, that
exposes other Playes, as the *Rebearsal*. *A Mock-holy-day*.
To Mock, or mimick another.

Moggy, in Scotch, as Peg in English, for Margaret.

Moil, to Drudge or Labour Hard. *To Moil and Toil*, to
Slave at it. *A Moiling Fellow*, a Drudge or great
Pains-taker.

Molinet, a Chocolate Stick, or little Mill.

Mongrel, c. a Hanger on among the Cheats, a Spunger. *Of a
Mongrel-race or Breed*, a Curr or Man of a base,
ungenerous Breed.

Mood, Humor. *In a merry Mood*, or good Humor; *in an ill
Mood*, or out of Humor. *Moody*, Humorous.

Moon-curser, c. a Link-boy, or one that under Colour of
lighting Men, Robs, them or leads them to a gang of
Rogues, that will do it for him.

Moon-men, c. Gipsies.

Moon-blind, a sort of Horses, weak-sighted.

Moppet, *a pretty Moppet*, a very pretty little Baby.

Mopsie, a Dowdy, or Homely Woman.

Mop-eied, one that can't see well, by living too long a Maid.

Mop'd, Maz'd.

Mopus, c. a half Penny or Farthing. *A meer Mopus grown*,
become dispirited, dull and Stupid.

Morglag, a Watch-man's brown Bill; as Glaives, are Bills or
Swords.

Morisco, a Morris or Morrice-dance, being belike some
Remains of a Moorish Custom with us, as the *Juego de
Toros*, or Feast of Bulls is, in *Spain*.

Mort, or Death, is Blown at the Death of the Deer.

Morts, c. Yeomen's Daughters; also a Wife, Woman, or
 Wench.

Moss-Troopers, so called from the Mosses, wast Lands in
 Lancashire, as the *Bog-Trotters* in *Ireland*, are from the
 Boggs there.

Mother, a Bawd.

Mother-midnight, a Midwife (often a Bawd.)

Mouchets, Patches for Ladies Faces.

Moveables, c. Rings, Watches, Swords, and such Toies of
 value. *As we bit all the Cull's Cole and Moveables*, c. we
 Won all the Man's Money, Rings, Watches, *&c. Very
 Moving*, prevailing, powerful, perswading.

Mountings, a Soldier's Arms and Cloths.

Mouse-trap. The Parsons Mouse-trap, Marriage. *He watcht me,
 as a Cat does a Mouse*, i.e. narrowly. *A Man or a Mouse*, a
 Prince or a Peasant. *A Mouse in the Pot is better than no
 Flesh*, or something has some Savour. *'Tis pitty to fling
 Water on a Drown'd Mouse*, or to depress the Miserable.
 A sorry Mouse, that has but one Hole, or a poor Creature
 that has but one Shift.

Mouth, a noisy Fellow. *A Mouthing Fellow*, a Bawling or
 scolding Person. *He never Speaks, but his Mouth opens.
 Mouth half Cockt*, gaping and staring at every thing they
 see.

Mower, c. a Cow.

Mow-heater, c. a Drover.

Muck, Money, Wealth; also Dung to manure Land.

Muckworm, a covetous Wretch.

Muckinder, a Child's Handkerchief tied by the side.

Muddled, half Drunk. *To Muddle on*, tho' so, yet to Drink
 on.

Muff, c. a Woman's Secrets. *To the well wearing of your Muff Mort*, c. to the happy Consummation of your Marriage Madam, a Health.

Muffling-cheat, c. a Napkin.

Muggletonians, the Sect or Disciples of *Lodowick Muggleton*.

Mulligrubs or *Mumps*, a Counterfeit Fit of the Sullens.

Mum-for-that, not a Word of the Pudding.

Mumble, to Mutter or Speak between the Teeth.

Mum-chance, one that sits mute. *He looks like Mum-chance that was Hang'd for saying of nothing.*

Mum-glass, the Monument, erected at the City-charge, in Memory of the dreadful Fire 1666, which consum'd the greatest Part of it.

Mumpers, c. Gentile-Beggers, who will not accept of Victuals, but Money or Cloths.

Mumpers-Hall, c. several Ale-houses in and about this City and Suburbs, in Allies, and By-places, much used by them, and resorted to in the Evening, where they will be very Merry, Drunk, and Frolicksom.

Mun-corn, half Wheat, half Rye.

Muns, c. the Face. *Touts his Muns*, c. note his Phis, or mark his face well.

Musick. It makes ill Musick, of any unwelcom or unpleasing News. *Touch that String most which makes best Musick*, or that cannot be Harped upon too often that pleases. *The Musick's paid*, c. the Watch-word among High-way-men, to let the Company they were to Rob, alone, in return to some Courtsey from some Gentleman among them.

Must, new Wine, or Wine on the Lea. *After Beef, Mustard*, of a thing preposterous, or out of Place; as we say, *the Cart before the Horse.*

Mute, when Hounds or Beagles run long without opening, or making any Cry; also a certain dumb Executioner among the *Turks*.

Muting, the Excrements of a Hern or Hawk.

Mutter, to Speak inwardly and between the Teeth.

Mutton-monger, a Lover of Women; also a Sheep-stealer.

Mutton-in-long-coats, Women. *A Leg of Mutton in a Silk-Stocking*, a Woman's Leg.

Muzzle, c. a Beard, (usually) long and nasty.

Myrmidons, c. the Constable's Attendants, or those whom he commands (in the King's Name) to Aid and assist him; also the Watch-men.

N

Nab, c. a Hat, Cap, or Head; also a Coxcomb. *I'll Nab ye*, c. I'll have your Hat or Cap. *Nim the Nab*, c. to Steal the Hat or Cap. *Nab'd*, c. Apprehended, Taken or Arrested.

Nab-cheat, c. a Hat.

Nab-girder, c. a Bridle.

Nanny-house, a Bawdy-house.

Nap, c. by Cheating with the Dice to secure one Chance; also a Clap, or Pox, and a short sleep. *Nap the Wiper*, c. to Steal the Handkerchief. *You have Napt it*, c. you are Clapt Sir. *To be caught Napping*, to be Surpriz'd, or Taken a sleep.

Napper, c. a Cheat, or Thief.

Napper of Napps, c. a Sheep-stealer.

Nappy-ale, very Strong, Heady.

N'are-a-face-but his own, Not a Penny in his Pocket.

Narrow, when the Biass of the Bowl holds too much. *'Tis all Narrow*, said by the Butchers one to another when their Meat proves not so good as expected. *A Narrow-soul'd Fellow*, poor or Mean-spirited, stingy. *Narrow or near search or Escape, watch him narrowly or nearly. Of a Narrow* or slender Fortune.

Nask, c. or *Naskin*, c. A Prison or Bridewell. *The old Nask*, c. the City Bridewell. *The new Nask*, c. Clerkenwell Bridewell. *Tuttle Nask*, c. the Bridewel in Tuttle-Fields. *He Napt it at the Nask*, c. he was Lasht at Bridewell.

Natural, c. a Mistress, a Wench; also a Fool.

Natural-children, Bastards.

Mr. *Nawpost*, a foolish Fellow.

Nay-word, a common By-word, or Proverb.

Nazie, c. Drunken.

Nazie-cove, c. a Drunkard.

Nazy-nabs, c. Drunken Coxcombs.

Neb, the Bill of a Bird, and the slit or point of a Pen. *She holds up her Neb*, she turns up her Snout to be Kist.

Neck-stamper, c. the Pot-Boy at a Tavern or Ale-house.

Neck-verse, a Favor (formerly) indulged to the Clergy only, but (now) to the Laity also, to mitigate the Rigor of the Letter of the Law, as in Man-slaughter, *&c.* Reading a Verse out of an old Manuscript Latin Psalter, (tho' the Book now used by the Ordinary is the same Printed in an old English Character) saves the Criminal's Life. Nay now even the Women (by a late Act of Parliament) have (in a manner) the benefit of their Clergy, tho not so much as put to Read; for in such Cases where the Men are allow'd it, the Women are of course sizz'd in the Fist, without running the risque of a Halter by not Reading.

Negro			Flat.
Hawk	*Nos'd,*		Hook'd.
Roman			Rais'd in the middle like *Kingston Bridge*.

Needle-point, c. a Sharper.

Neither-Vert, all sorts of Under-wood.

Neighborly, Friendly, Kind, Loving, Obliging. *You Live a great way off good Neighbors*, to him, that is the Trumpet of his own Praises.

Nestlings, Canary-Birds, brought up by Hand. *What a Nestling you keep*, how restless and uneasy you are. *Nest of Rabbets.*

Nettled, Teiz'd, provoked, made uneasy. *He has pist upon a Nettle*, he is very uneasy, or much out of Humor. *In Dock, out Nettle*, upon the change of Places, when one is no sooner out, but another is in his Place.

Nice, squeemish, precise. *More nice than wife*, *a Sir Courtly Nice*, a silly empty, gay, foolish Fellow.

Nickum, c. a Sharper; also a Rooking Ale-house or Innkeeper, Vintner, or any Retailer. *Nick it*, to win at Dice, to hit the Mark, to Drink the pin to, or button. *Old Nick*, the Devil. *Nick and Froth built the Pye at Aldgate*, sharping in the Reckonings and cheating in the Measure built that (once) Noted House.

Nickum-poop, a Fool, also a silly soft, Uxorious Fellow.

Nick-ninny, an empty Fellow, a meer Cod's Head.

Nig, c. the Clippings of Money.

Nigler, c. a Clipper.

Nigging, c. Clipping.

Nigling, c. accompanying with a Woman.

Night-Magistrate, a Constable.

Night-men, Gold-finders, Tom-turd-men.

Night-rale, a Woman's combing Cloth, to dress her Head in.

Night-walker, c. a Bell-man; also a Light Woman, a Thief, a Rogue.

Nigit, a Fool.

Nigmenog, a very silly Fellow.

Nikin, a Natural, or very soft creature; also Jsaac.

Nim, c. to Steal, or whip off or away any thing. *Nim a Togeman*, c. to Steal a Cloak. *Nim a Cloak*, c. to cut off the Buttons in a Crowd, or whip it off a Man's Shoulders.

Nim-gimmer, a Doctor, Surgeon, Apothecary or any one that cures a Clap or the Pox.

Ninny, c. a Canting whining Begger; also a Fool.

Ninny-hammer, a silly Senseless Fellow.

Nip, c. a Cheat; also to Pinch or Sharp any thing. *Nip a-bung*, c. to cut a Purse. *To Nip*, to Press between the Fingers and Thumb without the Nails, or with any broad Instrument like a pair of Tongs as to squeeze between Edged Instruments or Pincers. *Nipping Frost or Wind*, Sharp or Cutting. *To Nip in the Bud*, of an early Blast or Blite of Fruit; also to crush any thing at the beginning.

Nipperkin, c. half a Pint of Wine, and but half a Quartern of Brandy, Strong waters, *&c.*

Nipps, c. the Shears with which Money was won't to be Clipt.

Nit, wine that is brisk, and pour'd quick into a Glass; also a young Louse. *Nitts will be Lice.*

Nizy, c. a Fool, or Coxcomb.

Nob, c. a Head.

Nocky, c. a silly, dull Fellow.

Noddle, a Head.

Noddy, c. a Fool. *Knave-Noddy*, a Game on the Cards.

Nokes, a Ninny or Fool; also a noted Droll but lately Dead.

Nol, Oliver. *Old Nol*, the late Usurper *Cromwel*.

Noggin, (of Brandy) a Quarter of a Pint.

A Noble, six and eight-pence. *He has brought a Noble to Nine Pence*, of one that has reduced his Fortune.

Noise, used either of Harmonious or confused Sounds. *Noise of Thunder, or of a Mill, Noise of the Hounds, a Noise of Fiddles, of Trumpets and Drums, a Noise of Swords, or clashing; make a Noise Tom*, Hot Pudding-Pies.

Non-con, one that don't conform to the Church of *England*.

Nonjurors, Clergymen and others (Officers in the Army, Navy, *&c.*) That refus'd to take the Oaths to King *WILLIAM* and Queen *MARY*, and were turn'd out of their Livings and Employments.

Nooz'd, or *caught in a Nooze*, married; also Hanged.

Nose-gent, c. a Nun. *As plain as the Nose in your Face*, of a fair mark that cannot be hid. *He has a good Nose*, of a Smell-Feast. *He holds up his Nose*, of one that is Haughty, and carries his Head high. *He is led by the Nose*, of one that is easily imposed upon. *You make a Bridge of his Nose*, when you pass your next Neighbor in Drinking, or one is preferr'd over another's Head. *Follow your Nose*, said in a jeer to those that know not the way, and are bid to Smell it out, as we say to Smell a Post.

Nub, c. the Neck.

Nubbing, c. Hanging.

Nubbing-cheat, c. the Gallows.

Nubbing-Cove, c. the Hangman.

Nubbing-ken, c. the Sessions-house.

Nug, A Word of Love, as, *my Dear Nug*, my Dear Love.

Nugging-Dress, an odd or particular way, out of the Fashion.

Numms, c. a Sham, or Collar. Shirt, to hide the t'other when Dirty.

Num-skul, a Foolish Person.

Nut-crackers, c. a Pillory. *The Cull lookt through the Nut-crackers*, the Rogue stood in the Pillory.

O

Oaf, a Wise-acre, a Ninny or Fool, *Oafish* Silly.

Oak, *an Oak*, c. a rich Man, of good Substance and Credit.

Oats. *One that has sown his wild Oats*, or having run out of all, begins to take up and be more Staied.

Oberon. *King Oberon or little Oberon*, King of the Fairies.

Office, *His Office*, any Man's ordinary Haunt, or Plying-place, be it Tavern, Ale-house, Gaming-house or Bowling-green. *A cast of your Office*, or a Touch of your Employment. *Be good in your Office*, a Caveat to those that are apt to forget themselves in it.

Ogles, c. Eyes, *Rum Ogles*, c. fine, bright, clear, piercing Eyes.

Ogling, c. casting a sheep's Eye at Handsom Women. *The Gentry-mort has rum Ogles*, c. that Lady has charming black Eyes.

Old-Coney, after the first Year.

Old-dog-at-it, good or expert.

Old-dog-at-common-prayer, a Poor Hackney that cou'd Read, but not Preach well.

Old Harry, a Composition used by Vintners, when they bedevil their Wines.

Old-Mr-Gory, c. a piece of Gold.

Old Nick, the Devil.

Old Mob, a noted Hawker.

Old-Toast, a brisk old Fellow. *A pleasant Old Cuff*, a
frolicksom old Fellow.

Oliver's Skull, a Chamber-pot.

Olli-Compolli, c. the by-name of one of the principal Rogues
of the Canting Crew.

One in Ten, a Parson.

One of my Cosens, a Wench.

Open-Arse, a Medlar; also a Lewd Woman.

Open House, or Open Doors, free for all Comers or Goers.

Open-handed, *in Spending*, oppos'd to close-fisted. *Open in
Speech*, to reserv'd. *Open-Sea* when there is a free Trade,
oppos'd to a *Sea shut* up in War, by Pirates, Privateers
or Embargo's of Ships.

Opiniator, an Assuming positive Fellow, an obstinate felt-
conceited Coxcomb.

Orator to a Mountebank, the Doctor's Decoy who in
conjunction with Jack Pudding, amuses, diverts and
draws in the Patients.

Otter, an Amphibious Creature, betwixt a Beast and a Fish,
a great destroyer of Fish, affording much sport in
Hunting. *Otter watcheth*, Lodgeth. *Vent the Otter*,
Dislodge him. *An Otter whineth*, makes a noise at
Rutting time. *Hunteth for his Kind*, the Term for their
Copulation.

Over-vert, all manner of High Woods.

Over-sight, has two contrary Significations under one
Sound, for an *Oversight* is either the Care or Charge of,
or Inspection into any Affair, or else an *Oversight*

Imports a Slip or Error committed in it, for want of due
Care and Circumspection. *Over-shoes over Boots*, or to go
Through-stitch. *Overdo*, double Diligence.

*Oven, The Mother had never lookt for her Daughter in the Oven,
if she had not been there her self before, or, She muses as she
uses.*

Out-at-heels, or *Elbows*, in a declining Condition, going
down the Wind.

Out-run the Constable, to Spend more than is Got, or Run
out of an Estate, to run Riot.

Outside, that is the Outside, or utmost Rate.

Owlers, those who privately in the Night carry Wool to the
Sea-Coasts, near *Rumney Marsh* in *Kent* and some Creeks
in *Sussex &c.* and Ship it off for *France* against Law.

Oyl of Barley, strong Drink.

Ox-house. He must go through the Ox-house to Bed, of an old
Fellow that Marries a young Woman. *The black Ox has
not trod upon his Foot*, of one that has not been Pinch'd
with Want, or been Hard put to it.

P

Pack, a Fardel or Bundle. *Pack of Knaves, the worst of all the Pack*, or a Knave in Grain. *Pack of Juries, Packing of Cards, Pick a Pack, Pack up your Nawls and be gone*, Packing of Parties and Elections. *A common Pack-horse*, a Hackney or common Drudge, one made a Slave of.

Pad, c. the High Way, and a Robber thereon; also a Bundle. *Rum Pad*, c. a daring or stout High-way-man. *Paddington Fair*, c. an Execution of Malefactors at *Tyburn*; also a real Fair at the Village of that Name, near that Place. *Goes upon the Pad*, or a *Padding*, c. Robbs upon the Highway. *A Pad*, an easy Pacing Horse. *Padds*, worn by the Women to save their Sides from being Cut or Mark'd with the Strings of their Petty-coats.

Pageant, a thing Drest up and set out to make a Show. *A Piece of Pageantry*, a thing that makes a Figure in a Show or Play, as Play-house Kings and Generals Strut and Stalk upon the Stage.

Pain, not in Pain, not in Care or Concern.

Painter, the Rope that lies in the Ship's Long-boat, or Barge, alwaies ready to Fasten her, or Hale her on

Shoar. *I'll Cut your Painter for ye*, I'll prevent ye doing me any Mischief; the Tar-Cant, when they Quarrel one with another. *What pleases the Painter*, when any Representation in the Productions of his or any Art is unaccountable, and so is to be resolv'd purely into the good Pleasure of the Artist.

Pale of the Church, in or out of the Church's Enclosure.

Pall'd, Flat, Dispirited, or Dead Drink.

Pallet, a little Bed; also the Receiver of the Painter's Colours mingled, as the Shells are of his several Colours unmingled; also one half of the Pale in Heraldry.

Palm, the Attire of a Buck.

Paltry Fellow, a sorry, base, mean, contemptible Varlet.

Palliards, c. the Seaventh Rank of the Canting Crew, whose Fathers were Born Beggers, and who themselves follow the same Trade, with Sham Sores, making a hideous Noise, Pretending grievous Pain, do extort Charity.

Pam, the Knave of Clubbs.

Pamper'd $\begin{Bmatrix} Priest \\ Horse \end{Bmatrix}$ High-Fead.

Panam, c. Bread.

Pantas, a Disease in Hawks.

Panter, c. a Hart.

Pantry, Buttery.

Pantler, Butler.

Paper-Buildings, slight, Wooden, or old.

Paper-Skul, foolish, soft, silly.

Paper-Wars, Letter-combats.

Papers, Writings, or Deeds.

Paplar, c. Milk-pottage.

Par, Gold and Silver at a like Proportion.

Parasite, a Trencher-Friend, a meer Wheedle.

Parell, Whites of Eggs, Bay-Salt, Milk and Conduit-Water beat together, and poured into a Vessel of Wine to Cure it's Fretting, in order to Fine it, and make it Drink up.

Parse, to put By a Thrust or Blow.

Parings, c. the Clippings of Money.

Parlous, or *Perillous Man*, a notable, shrew'd Fellow.

Parsimonious, Near, Niggardly, Pinching, Stingy.

Pass, a Way, Lane, River, Leave; also condition. *What a Sad Pass things are come to?* In what an ill State they are. *That Shamm won't Pass*, that Trick won't take. *Do the Waters Pass well?* much in use at the Wells, do they Move as they ought? *To Passe upon one*, to top upon him, or impose upon him; also a Term at Billiards, when the Ball goes through the Court or Porch, it is said to pass.

Passage, a Camp-Game, with three Dice, Doublets, making up Ten or more, to *Pass* or Win, any other Chances lose.

Pass-bank, the Stock or Fund thereto belonging; also the playing Place Cut out in the Ground almost Cockpit waies.

Pat, apposite, or to the purpose.

Patering, the Maundring or pert Replies of Servants. *Patering of Prayers*, Muttering of them, from the thick Repeating of so many Paters or Pater-nosters. *No Penny, no Pater-nosters*, no Pay, no Prayers.

Patrico, c. or *Pater-cove*, c. the Fifeteenth Rank of the Canting Tribe, stroling Priests that Marry under a Hedge without Gospel or Common-prayer Book, the Couple standing on each side a Dead Beast, are bid to Live together till Death them do's Part, so shaking

Hands, the Wedding is ended; also any Minister, or Parson.

Pateepan, a little Pye, or small Pasty.

Patrole, the Rounds.

Paume, when a Die or Piece of Money is hid in the Hand, to secure the Game, or Wager. *He Paumes it*, he Cheats, or Plaies Foul.

Paw, a Hand.

Pawn, To Pawn any Body, to steal away and leave him or them to Pay the Reckoning.

Pay through the Nose, Excessively, or with Extortion.

Peak, c. any kind of Lace.

Pearls, the little Knobs on the Bur (which see) of a Stag.

Peck, c. Meat.

Peckidge, c. Meat. *Rum Peck*, c. good Eating. *The Gentry Cove tipt us rum Peck and rum Gutlers, till we were all Bowsy, and snapt all the Flickers*, the Gentleman gave us so much good Victuals, and Canary, that we were all Damn'd Drunk, and broke all the drinking Glasses.

Peculiars, Plants, Animals and Fossiles, proper and particular to some one Country, and rarely if ever found in others, as English Scurvy-grass, Sarsa, Sassafras and Guajacum, all West *Indian* Druggs; and so for Animals, English Maistiffs, Irish Grey-hounds, Barnacles, and *Soland* Geese peculiar to *Scotland*, as Puffins, to the Isle of *Man*; also Parishes exempt from other Ordinaries, and peculiarly belonging to the See of *Canterbury*.

Peculiar, c. a Mistress; also particular, private, proper.

Pedant, a meer Scholar, a School-master, a Man of one kind of Learning or Business, out of which he is good for nothing.

Pedantry, a Learning and Skill of one Colour.

Ped, a Basket.

Pedlars, Scotch Merchants; also English Retailers of Goods, that stroll from Town to Town.

Pedlars-French, a sort of Gibrish or made Language, easy to be Learnt and Understood, used by Gypsies, *&c.* Also the Beggers *Cant.*

Peeking Fellow, a meer Sneaks, one that peeps in every Hole and Corner; also a thin, weasel-faced Fellow.

Peeper, c. a Looking-glass. *Track the Dancers, and pike with the Peepers*, c. whip up the Stairs, and trip off with the Looking-glass.

Peepers, c. Eyes.

Peepy, c. *Peeping*, c. Drowsy, Sleepy. *As the Cull Peeps let's Mill him*, c. when the Man is a Sleep let's Kill him.

Peery, c. fearful, shy, sly. *The Cull's Peery*, c. the Rogue's afraid to venture.

Peeter, c. a Portmantle or Cloak-bag. *Bite the Peeter*, c. to whip off the Cloak-bag. *Biter of Peeters*, c. one that makes a Trade of whipping Boxes and Trunks from behind a Coach or out of a Waggon, or off a Horse's Back.

Pea-goose, a silly Creature.

Peg at Cocks, to throw at them at Shrovetide. *Gon to Pegtrantums*, Dead.

Pel-mel, helter-skelter.

Pelt, a Heat or Chafe. *What a Pelt you are in?* what a Chafe your in? Also the Dead Body of any Fowl the Hawk has killd.

Pelts, Beast Skinns.

Pelting-village, Blind, Obscure.

Penelope's Web, to do and undo.

Pennance-bord, c. a Pillory.

Pennites, that Faction of Quakers that follow most and are
in the Interest of *William Pen*, the chief Proprietor and
Governor of *Pensylvania*, a Country lying betwixt Forty
and Forty five Degrees of Latitude, in *America*, much
improv'd, and like to florish.

Penny-worth. I'll fetch my-Pennyworth out of him, or make him
earn what he cost me.

Penny-white, said of her, to whom Fortune has been kinder
than Nature. *Penny-wise and Pound-foolish*, Sparing in a
little and Lavish in a great Deal, *save at the Spiggot and
let it out at the Bunghole. A Penny-worth for one's Penny*,
for what is worth one's Money. *To get a Penny*, to
endeaver to Live; *to turn and winde the Penny*, to make to
most of one's Money, or Lay it out at the best
Advantage. *Pennyless*, poor, sharp, bare of Money.

Penurious, pinching, hard, parsimonious, little.

Pentice Nab, a very broad-brim'd Hat.

Pepperd off, Damnably Clapt or Poxt. *Pepper-proof*, not Clapt
or Poxt.

Pericranium, the Head or Skull.

Perking, the late D. of M.; also any pert forward silly
Fellow. *To Perk up*, to hold up the Head after Drooping.

Periwinkle, a Perruque or Periwig; also the same as
Pinpatches.

Pestilent-fine, Tearing-fine.

Pet, a Fret. *To be in a Pet*, or out of Humor.

Peter Lug, Who is Peter Lug? Who let's the Glass stand at
his Door?

Petrify, to turn to Stone.

Petrification, Concretions, either such as are hardned into
  Stone, by exposing them to Air, as Coral; or by casting
  them into Cold petrifying Waters, as Wood.

Pettycoat-Pensioner, a Gallant, or one Maintain'd for secret
  Service.

Phanatics, Dissenters from the Church of *England*.

Pharoah, very strong Mault-Drink.

Phenix-men, the same as *Fire-drakes*.

Philadelphians, a new Sect of Enthusiasts, pretenders to
  Brotherly Love, *&c.*

Philistines, Serjeants, Bailiffs and their Crew; also
  Drunkards. *I fell among the Philistines*, I chopt upon a
  knot of Drunken Fellows.

Phis, for *Physiognomy*, Face or Aspect.

Picking, little Stealing, Pilfering, petty Larceny.

Pickthank, a Tale-bearer, or an Insinuator by any means to
  curry Favor.

Pickaroon, a very small Privateer; also a shabby poor Fellow.

Pickled, very Arch or Waggish. *In Pickle*, Poxt. *Rodds in
  Pickle, or revenge in Lavender.*

Pig, c. Sixpence. *The Cull tipt me a Pig*, c. the Man gave me
  Sixpence.

Pig of the Sounder, see *Wild Boar*.

Pigsnie, word of Love.

Pig-widgeon, a silly Fellow.

Pike, c. to run away, flee, quit, or leave the Place; also to
  Die. *As he Pikes*, c. he walks or goes. *Pike on the been*, run
  away as fast as you can. *Piked off*, c. run away, fled,
  broke; also Dead, *To pass the Pikes*, to be out of Danger.

Pillau, a Hen and Rice Boil'd, a Turkish Dish, but now in
  use in *England*, *France* and *Holland*.

Pillory, a Baker; also Punishment mostly heretofore for Beggers, now for Perjury, Forgery and suborned Persons.

Pimp, the same as Cock-bawd.

Pimp-whisking, a Top Trader that way; also a little mean-spirited, narrow-soul'd Fellow.

Pimlico, a noted Cake-house formerly, but now converted into a Bowling green, of good report at *Hogsden* near *London*.

Pin, a small Vessel containing Four Gallons and a half, or the Eighth part of a Barrel. *To Pin himself upon you*, or to Hang on. *To Pin one's Faith on another's Sleeve*, or take all upon Trust, for Gospel that he saies. *Not a Pin to chuse*, when there is little or no difference. *Upon a merry Pin*, or in a pleasant Mood. *Nick the Pin*, to Drink fairly.

Pimginnit, a large, red, angry Pimple.

Pinch, to Steal, or Slily convey any thing away. *To Pinch*, to Cut the Measures of Ale, Beer, *&c*. *To Pinch on the Parson's side*, or Sharp him of his Tythes. *At Pinch*, upon a Push or Exigence.

Pinch-gut-hall, a noted House at *Milend*, so Nicknam'd by the *Tarrs*, who were half Starved in an *East-India* Voiage, by their then Commander, who Built (at his return) that famous Fabrick, and (as they say) with what he Pinch'd out of their Bellies.

Pinch-gut-money, allow'd by the King to the Seamen, that Serve on Bord the Navy Royal, when their Provision falls Short; also in long Voyages when they are forced to Drink Water instead of Beer.

Pinpatches, a small Shel-fish very like a Snail, but less,

Caught on the Ouzes at low Tide, in Rivers near the Sea, and Sold cheap.

Picquant, a sharp Reflection; also a poynant Sawce.

Pink't, Prickt with a Sword in a Rencounter or Duel. *He Pink'd his Doublet*, he Run him Through.

Piquet, a game at Cards.

Pit, c. the hole under the Gallows into which those that Pay not the Fee, *viz. 6s 8d*, are cast and Buried.

Pit-a pat, or *Pintle de Pantledy*, sadly Scared, grievously put to it.

Pitcher-bawd, the poor Hack that runs of Errands to fetch Wenches or Liquor. *Little Pitchers have large Ears*, Children may over-hear, and discover Secrets. *The Pitcher do's not go so often to the Well, but it comes home Broke at last*, of him that after many lucky Adventures or narrow Escapes, miscarries in the End.

Pithy jest, or Sentence, that couches a great deal in a little room.

Pittance, a small Largess or petty Gratuity.

Placaert, a Dutch Proclamation, or Order of the States.

Plad, Scotch striped Stuff.

Plaint for *Complaint*, *he made his Plaint to me*, or made his Complaint to me. Hence *Plaintiff* and *Defendant* at Law, for Complainant and Defendant.

Planks, thrown out to save those that can Swim in a Wreck; also Flooring.

Plant, c. to lay, place, or hide. *Plant your Whids and Stow them*, c. be wary what you say or let slip.

Plaister of hot Gutts, one warm Belly clapt to another.

Plate-fleet comes in, when Money comes to Hand.

Platter-fac'd-jade, a very broad, ord'nary faced Woman.

Plausible, smooth, specious, Taking.

Play it off, to play Booty; also to throw a way, at Gaming, so much and no more. *He Plaies it off*, he Cheats.

Pliant, supple, flexible, ductile, manageable, Wax to every Thumb.

Plodder, a Porer in Records, Writings or Books, a dull Drudge, or hard Student. *A Plodding Lawyer*, a Laborious Lawyer. *A Plodding Horse*, a good Drudge or Pack-horse.

Pluck the Ribond, or *Pluck Sir O——n*, ring the Bell at the Tavern.

Plump-in-the-pocket, flush of Money.

Plyer, c. a Crutch.

Poching, a sly destroying of Game, with Dogs, Netts, Snares *&c*. Contrary to the Laws; also an Egg Boyld in Water out of the Shell.

Poke, a Bag, Sack, or Pocket. *To buy a Pig in a Poke*, or unsight or unseen. *To carry your Passions in your Pocket*, or smother your Passions.

Poker, one that conveys Coals (at *Newcastle*) in Sacks, on Horse-back; also a pointed Porr to raise the Fire, and a Sword.

Polt on the Pate, a good Rap there.

Poltron, a Coward.

Ponyard, a short Dagger or Stilletto.

Porker, c. a Sword.

Porters, Hirelings to carry Burthens, Beasts of Burthen, or else Menial Servants set to Guard the Gates in a great Man's House, of whom Dr. *Donne* said pleasantly, that he was ever next the Door, yet the seldomest Abroad of any of the Family.

Portable, Pocketable.

Portage, Carriage of any thing, whether by Land or Water.

Posse Mobilitatis, the whole Rabble in a Body.

Post, Employment, Office, Station; also an advanced, or advantagious piece of Ground: A Pillar in the Way or Street. *From Pillar to Post*, from Constable to Constable.

Pot-hooks, Scrawls or bad Writing.

Pot-valiant, Drunk.

Pot and Spit, Boyl'd and Roast. *A little Pot is soon Hot*, of a little Fellow soon made angry. *The Pot calls the Kettle black A*——, when one accuses another of what He is as Deep in himself.

Poulain, a Bubo.

Powder-monkey, Boys planted at the Guns a Bord the Ship, to fetch Gun-powder *&c.* in the Engagement.

Powdring-Tub, the pocky Hospital at *Kingsland* near *London*.

Poyson'd, Big with Child.

Poyson-pate, red Hair'd.

Prancer, c. a Horse. *Prancers-nab*, c. a Horse's Head used in a Sham-Seal to such a Pass.

Prancers-poll, c. the same as before; also the Sign of the Nag's Head. *Mount the Prancer*, c. get on the Horse's Back.

Pranks, Tricks.

Pratts, c. Buttocks; also a Tinder-box or Touch-box.

Prating-cheat, c. a Tongue.

Prateroast, a Talking Boy.

Precarious, what is Disputable and uncertain, as being purely at the Pleasure and Courtesy of another.

Precaution, Forecast, or the Wisdom of Prevention, which is beyond that of Remedy.

Precipitate, Rass, Headstrong, Unadvised, Inconsiderate, hurrying in Business.

Precisians, Strait-laced, Squeemish, Foolishly Scrupulous.

Preservatives, Antidotes to keep off, or prevent Diseases.

Priest-craft, the Art of awing the People, managing their Consciences, and diving into their Purses.

Pretext, Show, Colour, Pretence, or Excuse.

Prey, c. Money.

Prick, the first Head of a Fallow Deer; also a Skewer.

Pricker, a Huntsman on Horse Back.

Pricketh, the Footing of a Hare on the hard Highway, when it can be perceived.

Prickear'd Fellow, a Crop, whole Ears are longer than his Hair.

Prick-louse, a Taylor.

Prickt, decayed Wine, tending to Sower. *The Prick and Praise of our Town*, that bears the Bell from all the Rest, in all Exercises, as Wrestling, Running, Leaping, Vaulting, Pitching of the Barr, *&c.*

Priest-link'd, Married.

Priest-ridden, wholly influenced, and absolutely govern'd by that Tribe.

Prig, c. a Thief, a Cheat; also a Nice beauish, silly Fellow, is called *a meer Prig*.

Priggs, c. the Ninth Rank of Canting Rogues, Thieves.

Priggers, c. Thieves.

Prigging, c. Riding; also Lying with a Woman.

Prigstar, c. a Rival in Love.

Priggish, c. Thievish.

Prig-napper, c. a Horse Stealer; also a Thief-taker.

Priggers of the Cacklers, c. Poultry-Stealers.

Priggers of Prancers, c. the Sixth Order of the Canting Crew,

Horse-Stealers, who carry a Bridle in their Pockets, a small Pad Saddle in their Breeches.

Primero, an old German Game at Cards.

Prim, a silly empty starcht Fellow.

Princock, a pert, forward Fellow.

Princes-metal, a mixt Metal, betwixt Brass and Copper, and of a mixt Colour between both, not so Pale as the one, nor so Red as the other, the late Invention of Prince *Rupert*.

Prince Prig, c. a King of the Gypsies; also a Top-Thief, or Receiver General.

Prinking, nicely Dressing. *Prinkt up*, set up on the Cupboards-head in their best Cloaths, or in State. Stiff-starched. *Mistress Princum-Prancum*, such a one.

Print, the Treading of a Fox. *To set in Print*, with Mouth skrew'd up and Neck Stretcht out.

Prisme, a Triangular Crystal-Glass or Fools Paradise, that by refraction reflects imaginary Blew, Red, and Yellow Colours upon all Objects seen through it; also any Saw-dust.

Prittle-Prattle, idle impertinent Chat.

Proclamations, his Head is full of Proclamations, much taken up to little Purpose.

Prog, c. Meat. *Rum Prog*, c. nice Eating. *The Cull tipt us Rum Prog*, c. the Gentleman Treated us very High.

Projectors, Busybodies in new Inventions and Discoveries, Virtuoso's of Fortune, or Traders in unsuccesful if not impracticable Whimms, who are alwaies Digging where there is no more to be found.

Proling, Hunting or Searching about in quest of a Wench, or any Game.

Property, a meer Tool, or Implement, to serve a Turn, a Cat's foot; also a natural Quality or Talent, and the highest right a Man can have to any thing, *Liberty and Property*, two Inestimable Jewells. To change the Property, or give it another turn, with a new Dress, or the Disguise of a Wig and a false Beard.

Proud Bitch, desirous of Copulation.

Prying Fellow, that is very curious to enquire into other Men's Secrets and Affairs.

Provender, c. he from whom any Money is taken on the Highway.

Puke, to Spue.

Pug, *Pugnasty*, *a meer Pug*, a nasty Slut, a sorry Jade, of a Woman; also a Monkey.

Puling, Sickly.

Pummel, the Hilt, Handle, or round Knob of a Sword, or Saddle; also to Beat. *I Pummel'd his Sides for him*, I Beat him soundly.

Pump, to wheedle Secrets out of any one; also to drench, Bailives, Serjeants, Pick-pockets, *&c. Pumpt dry*, not a Word left to say.

Pun, to Play with Words and Sounds.

Punch, Brandy and Water, with Limes or Lemon-juice; also a thick short Man. *Punch Nag*, a short, thick, fat, squat, strong Horse.

Punch-houses, Bawdy-houses.

Punchable, old passable Money, *Anno* 1695.

Punk, a little Whore.

Puny Child, weak little *Puny Stomack*. *Puny Judge*, the Junior or Youngest.

Pure, c. a Mistress.

Purest-pure, c. a Top-Mistress, or Fine Woman.

Pupil-mongers, Tutors at the Universities, that have many Pupils, and make a Penny of them.

Puritans, *Puritanical*, those of the precise Cut, strait-laced Precisians, *whining* (as Osborn saies) *for a Sanctity God never yet trusted out of Heaven.*

Purl, Worm-wood infus'd in Ale.

Purl-Royal, Canary with a dash of Worm-wood.

Pursenets, c. Goods taken upon Trust by young Unthrifts at treble the Value; also a little Purse.

Purse-proud, haughty because Rich.

Pursy, Foggy, Fat.

Pushers, Canary-birds new Flown that cannot Feed themselves.

Pushing-School, a Fencing School; also a Bawdy-house. *At a Push*, at a pinch or strait. *At Push of Pike*, at Defiance. *Push-pinn*, Children's Play. *To Push on one's Fortune*, to advance, or run it up.

Put. A Country-Put, a silly, shallow-pated Fellow. *Put to it*, Beset.

Q

Quacking-cheat, c. a Duck.

Quack, an Empirick, or meer pretender to Physic.

Quaffing, *Quaff off*, carousing, to carouse.

Quag, *Quagmire*, marshy moorish Ground.

Quailing of the Stomack, beginning to be qualmish or uneasy.

Quail-pipe, a Woman's Tongue; also a Device to take the Birds of that Name, which are fine Food, the French esteem'd the best; tho' both those and the English are of a Currish Nature, and will beat themselves against the Cage, sides and top, being with difficulty brought to Feed: Wheat is usually given them, but Hempseed is a great deal better.

Quaint, curious, neat; also strange.

Quaking-cheat, c. a Calf or a Sheep.

Qualified, Accomplisht, Statesman, Soldier, Scholar.

Qualifications, Accomplishments that render any of them Compleat; also Conditions.

Qually-Wines, Turbulent and Foul.

Qualm, a Stomack-Fit; also Calmness, and the Cry of Ravens.

Qualmish, Crop-sick, queasy Stomackt.

Quarrel-picker, a Glazier; also a contentious Fellow, a Trouble Company.

Quarron, c. a Body.

Quarte, Nails of the Sword-Hand quite up.

Quarting upon the streight Line, keeping the Head and Shoulders very much back from the Adversary's Sword, when one thrusts with his own.

Quash, to Suppress, Annul, or Overthrow. *To Quash the Indictment*.

Quean, a Whore, or Slut. *A dirty Quean*, a very Puzzel or Slut.

Queasy, Stomacht, Crop-sick, Qualmish.

Queen Elizabeth's Pocket-pistol, a Brass-Cannon of a prodigious Length at *Dover-Castle*.

Queere, base, Roguish, naught. *How Queerely the Cull Touts?* c. how roguishly the Fellow looks.

Queere Birds, c. such as having got loose, return to their old Trade of Roguing and Thieving.

Queere-bluffer, c. a sneaking, sharping, Cut throat Ale-house or Inn-keeper.

Queere-bung, c. an empty Purse.

Queere-clout, c. a sorry, coarse, ord'nary or old Handkerchief, not worth *Nimming*.

Queere cole, c. Clipt, Counterfeit, or Brass Money.

Queere cole-maker, c. a false-Coyner.

Queere cole-fencer, c. a Receiver and putter off false Money.

Queere-cove, c. a Rogue.

Queere-cuffin, c. a Justice of Peace; also a Churl.

Queere-cull, c. a Fop, or Fool, a Codshead; also a shabby poor Fellow.

Queere-degen, c. an Iron, Steel, or Brass-hilted Sword.

Queere-diver, c. a bungling Pick-pocket.

Queere-doxy, c. a jilting Jade, a sorry shabby Wench.

Queere-drawers, c. Yarn, coarse Worsted, ord'nary or old Stockings.

Queere-duke, c. a poor decayed Gentleman; also a lean, thin, half Starved Fellow.

Queere-fun, c. a bungling Cheat or Trick.

Queere-ken, c. an ill House, or a Prison.

Queere-mort, c. a dirty Drab, a jilting Wench, a Pockey Jade.

Queere-nab, c. a Felt, Carolina, Cloth, or ord'nary Hat, not worth whipping off a Man's Head.

Queere-kicks, c. coarse, ord'nary or old Breeches.

Queere-peepers, c. old-fashion'd, ord'nary, black-fram'd, or common Looking-glasses.

Queere-prancer, c. a Founder'd Jade, an ord'nary low-priz'd Horse.

Queere-topping, c. sorry Commodes or Head-dresses.

Quibble, to Trifle, or Pun. *Sir Quibble Queere*, a trifling silly shatter-brainn'd Fellow.

Quidds, c. Money. *Tip the Quidds*, c. can ye spend your Sixpence.

Quietists, a Numerous and considerable Sect amongst the Papists, being against Oral and wholly for Mental Prayer, Whiggs, Popish Precisians, or Puritans.

Quipps, Girds, Taunts, Jeers, *&c.*

Quirks in Law, Law-tricks or Subtleties.

Quirks and Quillets, Tricks and Devices.

Quod, c. Newgate; also any Prison, tho' for Debt. *The Dab's in the Quod*, c. the poor Rogue is in Limbo.

Quota, c. Snack, Share, Part, Proportion or Dividend. *Tip me my Quota*, c. give me my Part of the Winnings, Booty, Plunder, *&c.*

R

Rabbet-suckers, c. young Unthrifts taking up Goods upon Tick at excessive rates.

Rabbet, the first Year.

Rabbits, Wooden Kanns to Drink out of, once used on the Roads now, almost laid by.

Rabble, the Mob.

Racket, a Noise or Bustle; also Tennis-play. *What a Racket those Ramps keep?* What a busel these rude Children make?

Racking of Wines, Drawing them off their Lees into fresh Vessels.

Rack-rent, strain'd to the utmost Value. The Knights of *Cales*, Gentlemen of *Wales*, and Lairds of the *North Country*, a Yeoman of *Kent*, at Rack-rent, will buy 'em all Three. *To lye at Rack and Manger*, to live hard.

Rag, c. a Farthing. *Not a Rag left*, c. I have Lost or Spent, all my Money.

Ragou, a Relishing Bit, with a high Sawce.

Ragamuffin, a Tatterdemallion.

Rag-water, a common sort of Strong-waters.

Rake, Rake Hell, Rake-shame, a Lewd Spark or Deboshee, one
that has not yet Sowed his Wild Oats. *Rakish*, tending
to, or leaning towards that Extravagant way, of Life.
Rake, when the Hawk flies out too far from the Fowls;
also so much of the Ship's Hull as overhangs both Ends
of the Keel; and to Trot a Horse gently.

Ralph-Spooner, a Fool.

Raillery, Drolling. *To Railly*, or Droll. *A Railleur*, or Droll.

Rally, to Unite or embody broken Troops.

Rammish, Rank.

Ramp, a Tomrig, or rude Girl. *To Ramp*, to Play rude
Horse-Play.

Rampant, uppish, over-bold, over-pert, over-lusty. *A Lyon
Rampant*, i. e. rearing up his Fore-feet.

Rangle, when Gravel is given to a Hawk, to bring her to a
Stomack.

Ranging, c. intriguing, and enjoying many Women.

Rank, rammish, strong-scented, as all the Fetids, either
Vegetables or Animals, as Garlick, Assa fœtida,
Polecats, Foxes, Goats, *&c.* And whatever is Stale,
Corrupt, or Tainted, and Stinks with long or careless
Keeping. *A Rank Lie*, a lewd or flat Lie. *A Rank Knave*,
an errant base Knave. *A Rank Whore*, an errant Whore.

Rank-rider, c. a High-way-man, also a Jockey.

Rank-wink'd, Hawk, that is a slow Fligher.

Rant, to Talk Big, High, or Boast much.

Ranters, Extravagants, Unthrifts, Lewd Sparks; also of the
Family of Love.

Rantipole, a rude Wild Boy or Girl.

Rap, to Swop or Exchange a Horse or Goods; also a Polt on
the Pate, and a hard Knocking at a Door.

Rapparies, Wild Irish Robbers, and Out-laws.

Rapper, a swinging great Lie.

Raree-show-men, poor *Savoyards* strolling up and down with portable Boxes of Puppet-shews at their Backs; in short, Pedlars of Puppets.

Rascal, a base, vile Fellow, a Rogue.

Rascal-Deer, lean, poor, *out-lying Deer*.

Rat, a Drunken Man or Woman taken up by the *Watch*, and carried by the Constable to the Counter. *To smell a Rat*, to suspect a Trick.

Rattler, c. a Coach.

Rattling-cove, c. a Coach-man.

Rattling Mumpers, c. such Beggers as Ply Coaches. *To Rattle*, c. to move off or be gone. *We'll take Rattle*, c. we must nor tarry, but whip away.

Rattling, the Noise of Coaches and Carts, as also of Armour, or of Hail, or Thunder.

Rattle-pate, a Hot, Maggot-pated Fellow. *I Rattled him*, I Rated him roundly, and told him his own.

Rattleth, the Noise a Goat maketh at Rutting-time.

Ravilliac, any Assassin.

Raw-head and Bloody-bones, a Bull-begger or Scare-child.

Rayn-deer, a Beast like a *Hart*, but has his Head fuller of Antlers.

Ready, c. *Ready and Rhino*, c. Money in Possession.

Rebel-rout, the, Rabble, running Riot.

Reaking, smoking or piping-hot, as Pies out of the Oven, Iron out of the Forge, or Blood from a warm Wound. Hence perhaps the *Reck*, or *Reaking*, i. e. Smoak of the Clouds, *I'll Reak my Spite on him*, I'll be Revenged on him.

Rear the Boar, Dislodge him.

Rebus's, Words or Sentences that are the same backwards as forwards.

Recheat, a Lesson blown on the Horn.

Recorder, a musical Instrument; also a Law-Officer or Magistrate in Cities and Corporations, their Mouth, or Spokesman.

Recreant, a Poltron, or Coward, one that eats his Words, or unsaies what he said.

Recruits, c. Money (Expected.) *Have you rais'd the Recruits*, c. is the Money come in?

Red-fustian, Clarret or red Port-Wine.

Red-letter-man, a Roman-catholic.

Red-rag, a Tongue. *Your Red-rag will never lie still*, your Tongue will ne're be quiet.

Red-shank, c. a Duck.

Refugies, French and Vaudois Protestants, forced to quit their own and fly into others Countries to have the Excercise of their Religion.

Refreshed, either as the Air is with Winds, when it Blows a Fresh Gale; or artificially with the motion of Fanns, or opening the Windows to Fann a close Room; or as Wines are with Snow and Ice; or by casting a new Gloss, on what is worn out, Withered, or Decayed, in Bodies Artificial, as Embroidery by Burnishing, or of Pictures by Varnishing, *&c.*

Rellif, Copulation of Hares.

Remember Parson Malham, (Norfolk) Pray Drink about Sir.

Regraters, Fore-stallers in Markets.

Repartee, a sudden smart Reply.

Republican, a Common-wealths-man.

Reserve, a Store or Hoard to have recourse to, upon a Push or particular Exigence; a Nest-Egg.

Respost, having given a Thrust, to Receive one from the Adversary, before he has recover'd his Body.

Resty, Head-strong, Wayword, Unruly, Masterless.

Retailers, Parcel-traders or Dealers, petty Merchants, Hucksters, Chandlers, Pedlars, *&c. In Retail*, in Parcel or small Sum, oppos'd to what goes in Tale or Sum at Large.

Retainers, a Great Man's Followers or Servants, attending him (heretofore) in Blew Coats and Badges, which were the Ancient Liveries, tho' little more remains of it at present, save what is left among the Water-men. Hence the Word *Retinue*, or Train of Attendance.

Revers'd, c. a Man set (by Bullies) on his Head, and his Money turn'd out of his Breeches.

Reward, what is given the Hounds, or Beagles by the Hands of the Hunts-man or others, after they have finished their Chase, by the Death of what they pursu'd.

Rhino, c. ready Money.

Rhinocerical, c. full of Money. *The Cull is Rhinocerical*, c. the Fop is full of Money.

Rib, or Ribroasting, a Dry-basting.

Ribbin, c. Money. *The Ribbin runs thick*, c. his Breeches are well lined with Money. *The Ribbin runs thin*, c. he has but little Cash about him.

Richess, (of Marterns) a Company.

Rich-face, a Red-face.

Ridg-cully, c. a Gold-smith.

Riff-raff, the Rabble or Scum of the People, Tagrag and Long-tail.

Ridge, or *row of Hills*, extended in a Line.

Ridicule, to Railly or turn any thing to a Jest. *To turn it all to Ridicule*, to make a Mock of it.

Rigging, c. Cloaths. *I'll Unrig the Bloss*, c. I will Strip the Wench. *Rum Rigging*, c. fine Cloaths. *The Cull has Rum Rigging, let's Ding him, and Mill him, and Pike*, c. the Man has very good Cloths, let us Knock him Down, Rob him, and Scour off.

Rill, a Rivulet, or small River.

Ring, c. Money extorted by Rogues on the High-way, or by Gentlemen Beggers. *A Ring*, a Concourse of People for Wrestling, Cudgel-playing, &c. *A Ring of Hills*, a round Circle of Hills.

Ring-walks, the Dew-rounds made by Hunts-men, when they go drawing in their Springs at Hart-Hunting.

Ripe, ready, come to maturity. *Matters are not Ripe*, not ready, or come to Perfection.

Riveted, or *Rooted* Customs, or Habits; inveterate or confirmed Diseases.

Roam, to wander far and wide from Home.

Roberds-men, c. the third (old) Rank of the Canting Crew, mighty Thieves, like *Robin-hood*.

Rochester-portion, two torn Smocks, and what Nature gave.

Roe. A Fair Roe-buck, the fifth Year; *a Roe-buck of the first Head*, the fourth Year; *a Hemuse*, the third Year; *a Gyrle*, the second Year; *a Kid*, the first Year; *a Roe Beddeth*, Lodgeth; *a Roe Belloweth*, maketh a Noise at Rutting time.

Roger, c. a Portmantle, a Goose; also a Man's Yard.

Rogues, c. the fourth Order of Canters. *A Rogue in Grain*, a very great Rogue. *A Great-he-rogue*, a sturdy swinging Rogue.

Romance, a feigned pleasant History. *To Romance*, to Lie pleasantly, to Stretch in Discourse.

Romboyles, c. Watch and Ward.

Romboyl'd, c. sought after with a Warrant.

Romer, a drinking glass; also wider.

Rook, c. a Cheat, a Knave. *To Rook*, c. to Cheat or play the Knave.

Rope. *Upon the High-ropes*, Cock-a-hoop. *Give him Rope enough and he'll Hang himself*, he'll Decoy himself within his own Destiny.

Rosy-gills, c. Sanguine or fresh-colour'd.

Rost-meat-cloths, Holiday-cloths. *You cannot fare well, but you must cry Rost-meat*, you can't meet with good Chear, but you must tell Tales. *To give one Rost-meat, and Beat him with the Spit*, to do one a Curtesy, and Twit or Upbraid him with it. *To rule the Rost*, to be Master, or Paramount. *Roasted*, Arrested. *I'll Roast the Dab*, I will Arrest the Rascal.

Rot-gut, very small or thin Beer.

Rovers, Pirates, Wanderers, Vagabonds. *To Shoot at Rovers*, at Random. *To Rove about*, to wander idly up and down.

Rough, Unpolisht, Unmannerly, Uncouth. *To lie Rough*, in one's Clothes all Night.

Round-dealing, Plain, Honest Dealing.

Round-summ, a Lusty-Summ.

Round-heads, the Parliamentarian Party in the great Rebellion, that begun 1641.

Rout, (of Wolves) a Company.

Rouse, (the Buck) Dislodge him.

Rawland-for-an-Oliver, to give as good as he brought.

Roysters, c. rude, Roaring Rogues.

Rub, c. to Run away. *A Rub*, an Impediment, Obstacle, Hinderance, Stop, or Difficulty. *Rub on*, to Live Indifferently. *Rub'd off*, c. Broke, and run away. *Rub through the World*, to Live Tollerably well in it.

Rubbers, Two (and sometimes Three) Games to make up; also a Rencounter with drawn Sword, and Reflections made upon any one.

Rub-rub, us'd on Greens when the Bowl Flees too fast, to have it forbear, if Words wou'd do it.

Rub-up, or refresh the Memory.

Rub-up, or Scower Armour, *&c.*

Rubs us to the Whit, c. sends us to Newgate.

Ruby-face, very red.

Ruck, a Bumble, or Heap.

Rud, a small Fish with a forked Tail, between which and the Roach, there is much about the same difference, as between the Herring and the Pilchard.

Ruff, an old-fashioned double Band; also a noted Bird, and a Fish, Pope, like a small Pearch, and when the Hawk hits the Prey, and yet not Trusses it.

Ruffin, c. the Devil; also a Justice of Peace, and also an Assasin.

Rufflers, c. the first Rank of Canters; also notorious Rogues. *To Ruffle*, to disorder any thing.

Ruff-mans, c. the Woods or Bushes.

Ruff-peck, c. Bacon. *As the Ruffin nab the Cuffin queere, and let the Harmanbeck Trime with his Kinchins about his Colquarron*, c. let the Devil take Justice, and let the Constable Hang with his Children about his Neck.

Ruffter-hood, a plain and easy Leather-hood worn by a
   Hawk, when first drawn.

Rug. It's all Rug, c. the Game is secured.

Rum, c. gallant, Fine, Rich, best or excellent; also a West-
   Indian Drink stronger than Brandy; drawn from Dreggs
   of Sugar for the most part, yet sometimes from Fruits,
   and Rows of Fish; best when old, much us'd in Punch.

Rumly, c. bravely, cleaverly, delicately, &c.

Rum-booze, c. Wine; also very good or strong Drink.

Rum-boozing-Welts, c. bunches of Grapes.

Rum-beck, c. any Justice of the Peace.

Rum-bob, c. a young Prentice; also a sharp, sly Trick, and a
   pretty short Wig.

Rum-bite, c. a cleaver Cheat, a neat Trick.

Rum-bleating-cheat, c. a very fat Weather.

Rum-blower, c. a very Handsom Mistress, kept by a
   particular Man.

Rum-bluffer, c. a jolly Host, Inn-keeper, or Victualler.

Rum-bughar, c. a very Pretty and Valuable Dog.

Rum-bung, c. a full Purse.

Rum-bubber, c. a cleaver or dextrous Fellow at Stealing
   Silver-Tankards (formerly) from Publick House.

Rum-cod, c. a good Purse of Gold, or round Summ of
   Money.

Rum-cove, c. a great Rogue.

Rum-cul, c. a rich Fool, that can be easily *Bit*, or Cheated
   by any body; also one that is very generous and Kind
   to a Mistress, and as

Rum-chub, c. which is (among the Butchers) one that is
   easily perswaded to believe what they say of the
   Goodness, and also to give them an extraod'nary Price

for their Meat, a very ignorant Market-man or Woman, that Laies out a great deal of Money with, and is *Bit* by them.

Rum-clout, c. a silk, fine Cambrick, or Holland Handkerchief.

Rum-cole, c. new Money, or Medals, curiously Coyn'd.

Rum-dropper, c. a Vintner.

Rum-duke, c. a jolly handsom Man.

Rum-dutchess, c. a jolly handsom Woman. *Rum-dukes*, c. the boldest or stoutest Fellows (lately) amongst the *Alsatians, Minters, Savoyards, &c.* Sent for to remove and guard the Goods of such Bankrupts as intended to take Sanctuary in those Places.

Rum-doxy, c. a Beautiful Woman, or light Lady.

Rum-degen, c. a Silver-hilted or inlaid Sword.

Rum-dell, c. as *Rumdoxy*.

Rum-diver, c. an compleat, or cleaver Pick-pocket.

Rum-drawers, c. Silk Stockings, or very fine Worsted Hose.

Rum-dubber, c. an experienc'd or expert Picker of Locks.

Rumford-Lyon, a Calf.

Rum-fun, c. a cleaver Cheat, or sharp Trick.

Rum-file, c. as *Rum-diver*.

Rum-gutlers, c. Canary-Wine.

Rum-glymmar, c. King or Chief of the Link-boies.

Rum-ghelt, c. as *Rum-cole*.

Rum-hopper, a Drawer. *Rum-hopper, tip us presently a Boozing-cheat of Rum-gutlers*, c. Drawer fill us presently a Bottle of the best Canary.

Rum-kicks, c. Silver or Gold Brocade Breeches, or very rich with Gold or Silver Galoon.

Rum-mawn'd, c. one that Counterfeits himself a Fool.

Rum-mort, c. a Queen, or great Lady.

Rum-nab, c. a Beaver, or very good Hat.

Rum-ned, c. a very silly Fellow.

Rum-nantz, c. true French Brandy.

Rum-pad, c. the High-way.

Rum-padders, c. the better sort of Highway-men, well Mounted and Armed.

Rum-peepers, c. a Silver Looking-glass.

Rump-and-Kidney-Men, c. Fidlers that play at Feasts, Fairs, Weddings, *&c*. And Live chiefly on the Remnants, of Victuals.

Rumbling, the rolling of Thunder, motion of a Wheelbarrow, or the noise in the Gutts.

Rum-prancer, c. a very beautiful Horse.

Rum-quidds, c. a great Booty, or large Snack.

Rum-ruff peck, c. Westphalia-Ham.

Rum-squeeze, c. much Wine or good Liquor given among the Fidlers.

Rum-snitch, c. a good fillip on the Nose.

Rum-tol, c. as *Rum-degen*, the newest Cant of the two.

Rum-tilter, c. as *Rumtol*.

Rum-topping, c. a rich commode or Head-dress.

Rum-ville, c. *London*.

Rum-wiper, c. as *Rum-clout*.

Run-ryot, to turn Spark, and run out of all; also when Hounds run at a whole Herd of Deer.

Running-stationers, Hawkers, or those that cry News and Books about the Streets.

Runt, a little, short, truss Man or Beast.

Runts, Canary-Birds above three Years old.

Runner, c. as *Budge*; also a Galley, or nimble Vessel, to make quick Voyages, as also to escape Privateers, Pirates, *&c.*

Rup, a filthy Boil, or Swelling on the Rump of Poultry, Corrupting the whole Body, Cured with Salt and Water.

Rustic, a clownish Country Fellow.

Rustygutts, an old blunt Fellow.

Rutt, Copulation (of Deer.)

S

Sack, c. a Pocket. *Dive into his Sack*, c. to Pick his Pocket.

Sails, Hawk's Wings; also Windmill-wings. *How you Sail about?* How you Santer about?

Salamander, a Bomb-vessel; also a certain Creature (said) to Live in the Fire, and a Stone (lately) found in *Pensylvania* full of Cotton, which will not (as a modern Author affirms) consume in the Fire; and a red-hot Iron to light Tobacco with.

Sales-men, Brokers who sell Cattel for the Graziers to the Butchers, before, and at the Beast-Market; also Sellers of ready-made Cloaths.

Salesman's-dog, the same as *Barker*.

Sally, a fit of Passion, or Humor.

Salmon, c. the Beggers Sacrament or Oath.

Salt, Lecherous, Proud. *To come after with Salt and Spoons*, of one that is none of the Hastings.

Salt-eel, a Rope's end used to Drub the Boies and Sailors on board of Ship.

Salvages, Barbarous People, Inhabiting near the Sea-Coasts in the Maritim Counties, who make a Prey of what the

Sea has (in Pity) spared, Living upon the Spoil of Ship-wrecks.

Samlets, so called the Spring following after they are Spawn'd, and tho' then but a little bigger than a Minnow, will (as Authors say) grow to be a Salmon in as short a time as a Goslin will to be a Goose.

Sandy-pate, one red-hair'd.

Sap-pate, a Fool.

Saunter, to loiter Idly, a Term borrowed from those Religious Counterfeits, who under the colour of Pilgrimages, to the *Holy Land*, us'd to get many Charities, crying still, *Sainct terre, Sainct terre*, having nothing but the Holy Land in their Mouths, tho' they stay'd alwaies at Home.

Saucy, impudent, bold. *More sauce than Pig. Your Sauce-Pan runs over*, you are exceeding bold.

Sawny, a Fool. *He's a meer Sawny*, he is very soft, tho' (in Scotch) it is only for Alexander.

Scab, a sorry Wench, or Scoundril-Fellow.

Scamper, c. to run away, or Scowre off, either from Justice, as Thieves, Debtors, Criminals, that are pursued; or from ill fortune, as Soldiers that are repulst or worsted.

Scandalous, c. a Periwig.

Scandal-proof, a thorough pac'd *Alsatian*, or *Minter*, one harden'd or past Shame.

Shift the Scene, call a new Cause, or change the Discourse.

School-butter, a Whipping. *I School'd him*, I chid him severely.

School of Venus, c. a Bawdy-house.

Sconce, to build a large Sconce, to run deep upon Tick, or Trust.

Scotch-hobby, a little sorry, scrubbed low Horse of that Country.

Scotch-mist, a sober, soaking Rain.

Scoundrel, a Hedge-bird or sorry Scab.

Scoure, c. to wear. *To Scoure the Cramp-rings*, c. to wear Bolts.

Scout, c. a Watch.

Scowre, c. to run away or scamper. *Let us Scowre, or we shall be Boned*, c. let us run away or we shall be Taken.

Scowrers, c. Drunkards, beating the Watch, breaking Windows, clearing the Streets, *&c.*

Scrip, c. a shred or scrap of Paper. *As the Cully did freely blot the Scrip, and tipt me 40 Hogs*, c. one enter'd into Bond with me for 40 Shillings.

Scrub, a Ragamuffin.

Scrubado, the Itch.

Scrape-all, a Money Scrivener; also a miserable Wretch, or griping Fellow.

Screw, *to Screw one up*, to exact upon one, or Squeeze one in a Bargain or Reckoning.

Scud, the course or motion of the Clouds, in Fleeting.

Scud-away, to Sail, Ride, or Run very fast.

Scumm, the Riff-Raff, or Tagrag and Longtail. *Rake Hell and Skim the Devil.*

Scut, the Tail of a Hare or Coney.

Scuttle, to run away; also a square hole to go down through the Deck.

Sealer, c. one that gives Bonds and Judgments for Goods and Money.

Season of Beasts, a Hart or Buck begins at the end of Fencer-Month, 15 Days after Midsummer-day, and lasteth till Holyrood-day. The Fox till Christmass, and lasteth till the Annunciation of the blessed Virgin. The Hinde or Doe at Holyrood-day, till Candlemass. The Roe-buck at

Easter, till Michaelmas. The Roe at Michaelmas till Candlemass. The Hare at Michaelmas, till the end of *February*. The Wolf from Christmas, till the Annunciation of the blessed Virgin. The Boar at Christmass, and continues to the Purification of our Lady.

Second-sighted, such as (they say) can, and do see Spirits, Apparitions, *&c*.

Secret, *let into the Secret*, c. when one is drawn in at Horse-racing, Cock-fighting, Bowling, and other Sports or Games, and *Bit*.

Seeling, when a Hawk first taken, is so blinded with a Thred run through the Eye-lids, that she Seeth not, or very little, the better to make her endure the Hood; also a sudden healing forced by the motion of the Sea or Wind.

Seraglio, a Bawdy-house; also the Great Turk's Palace.

Seraglietto, a lowsy, sorry Bawdy-house, a meer Dog-hole.

Setters, or *Setting-dogs*, they that draw in *Bubbles*, for old Gamesters to Rook; also a Sergeant's Yeoman, or Bailiff's Follower, or Second, and an Excize Officer to prevent the Brewers defrauding the King.

Sewet, Deer's Grease.

Shabby, in poor, sorry Rigging.

Shabberoon, a Ragamuffin.

Shab'd-off, sneakt, or slid away.

Shaftsbury, a Gallon-pot full of Wine, with a Cock.

Shag-bag, a poor, shabby Fellow.

Shallow-pate, a foolish silly, empty Fellow.

Sham, c. a Cheat, or Trick. *Cut a Sham*, c. to play a Rogue's Trick.

Shamble-Legg'd, one that goes wide, and shuffles his Feet about. *Shake your Shambles*, haste, begon.

Shameless, a bold forward Blade.

Shanks, Leggs. *There's Shanks!* there's ill Leggs.

Shanker, a little Scab or Pox on the Nut or Glans of the Yard.

Shappeau, c. or *Shappo*, c. for *Chappeau*, a Hat, the newest Cant, *Nab* being very old, and grown too common.

Shapes, said (often) to an ill-made Man. *Show your Shaper*, turn about, march off, be gone. *Great in more Shapes*, great in more Professions, or Capacities. *Great in all Shapes*, great in all the Branches of any one, or more Professions: As, great in all the Parts or Branches of the Law; (an universal Lawyer) Great in all the Parts or Branches of Learning, (an universal Scholar).

Shark, c. a Sharper; also a Large voracious Fish.

Sharper, c. a Cheat, one that Lives by his Witts.

Sharp, subtil, ready, quick, forward, of Lively Apprehension; also Poor and Needy.

Sharpers-tools, c. False Dice.

Sharp-set, very Hungry.

Shaver, a Cunning Shaver, a subtil, smart Fellow. *He Shaves close*, he gripes, squeezes, or extorts very severely.

Shavings, c. the Clippings of Money.

She is with Cub, when the Fox hath Young ones in her.

She-napper, c. a Woman Thief-catcher; also a Cock, (he) or Hen (she) Bawd, a Procuress and Debaucher of young Virgins; a Maiden-head-jobber.

Sheep-biter, a poor, sorry, sneaking, ill-lookt Fellow.

Sheepish, (Fellow) bashful, peaking.

Sheep's-head, a Fool, a Block-head.

Sheep-shearers, c. Cheats.

Shie, coy, squeamish, cold, or averse.

Shock, a Brunt. *To stand the Shock*, to bear the brunt.

Shocking, what is offensive, grating, grievous.

Shop, c. a prison.

Shopt, c. imprison'd.

Shop-lift, c. one that Steals under pretence of Cheap'ning.

Shoe-makers-stocks, pincht with strait Shoes. *No Man knows where the Shoe pinches but he that wears it*, or another's Cross like him that bears it. *Who goes worse Shod than the Shoe-maker's Wife? One Shoe will not fit all Feet*, Men are not all of a Size, nor all Conveniences of a Last. *To throw an old Shoe after one*, or wish them good Luck in their Business.

Short-pots, false, cheating Potts used at Ale-houses, and Brandy-shops.

Shot, *Shotlings*, large, lean Piggs bought to fatten. *To Pay one's Shot*, to Pay one's Club or Proportion.

Shot 'twixt Wind and Water, Clapt, or Poxt.

Shoulder-clapper, c. a Sergeant or Bailiff.

Shoulder-sham, c. a Partner to a File.

Shove the Tumbler, c. to be Whipt at the Cart's Tail.

Shred, a Tailer.

Shrieketh, the Noise a Badger makes at Rutting Time.

Shrouds, burying cloths, (now) Woollen, (anciently) Linnen; also Steps or Ladders (on board of Ship) to go up to the Topps.

Shuffler, a Bird like, but not so big as a Duck, having a broader Bill.

Shuffling-Fellow, a slippery, shifting, Fellow.

Shurk, c. a Sharper.

Sice, c. Six pence.

Sickrel, a puny, sickly Creature.

Siege, a Stool to set upon; also used by Physicians to their Patients. *How many Sieges have you had?* i.e. How many Stools have you had? Upon taking a Purge *&c.*

Simkin, a Fool.

Simon, c. Six-pence.

Simples, Follies, also Plants or Physical Herbs. *He must be cut of the Simples*, Care must be taken to cure him of his Folly.

Simpleton, a silly Creature, or Tony.

Single, the Tail of a Hart, Buck or other Deer.

Singler, or *Sanglier*, *a* wild Boar after the 4*th* Year.

Single-ten, a very foolish, silly Fellow; also Nails of that size.

Sir John, the Country-Vicar or Parson.

Sir Timothy, one that Treats every Body, and Pays the Reckonings every where.

Six and eight-pence, c. the usual Fee given, to carry back the Body of the Executed Malefactor, to give it Christian Burial.

Skew, c. a Begger's Wooden Dish. *To look a Skew*, or on one side.

Skew-fisted, awkward, ungainly.

Skin-flint, a griping, sharping, close-fisted Fellow.

Skinker, that fills the Glass or Cup. *Who Skinks?* Who pours out the Liquor.

Skipper, c. a Barn; also a Dutch Master of a Ship or Vessel.

Skip-jacks, c. youngsters that Ride the Horses for Sale.

Skip-kennel, a Foot-boy, or Laquais.

Slam, c. a Trick; also a Game entirely lost without getting one on that side.

Slat, c. a Sheet.

Slate, c. a half Crown.

Sleeping House, without Shop, Ware-house, or Cellar, only for a private Family.

Sleeveless-errand, such as Fools are sent on, the first of April.

Sleeveless-story, a Tale of a Tub, or of a Cock and a Bull. *To laugh in one's Sleeves*, inwardly slyly.

Slice, when a Hawk *Muteth* a great distance from her.

Slippery Trick, or Fellow, deceitful, as having two properties of Ice, smooth and slippery.

Slot, the footing of a Hart.

Slough, a deep miry Hole.

Slubber'd over, Work slightly wrought, or huddled up in haste.

Slubber-degullion, a slovenly, dirty, nasty Fellow.

Slug, a drone, or dull Tool; also a Bullet, beat into another Shape.

Slur, c. a Cheat at Dice; also a slight Scandal or Affront.

Sly-boots, a seeming Silly, but subtil Fellow.

Smack, a Tang, or ill Taste.

Smacking-cove, c. a Coachman.

Smart-money, given by the King, when a Man in Land or Sea-Service has a Leg Shot or Cut off, or is disabled.

Smart, witty, sharp; also pain.

Smatterer, one half-learned. *A Smattering*, a slight Tincture in any Skill or Learning.

Smeller, c. a Nose.

Smelling-cheat, c. a Nose-gay; also an Orchard or Garden.

Smelts, c. half Guineas. *Tip me a Smelt*, c. Prithee lend me half a Guinea.

Smirk, a finical, spruce Fellow. *To Smirk*, to look pleasantly.

Smiter, c. an Arm.

Smash, c. to kick down Stairs. *The Chubbs, toute the Blosses, they Smash, and make them brush*, c. the Sharpers catch their Mistresses at the Tavern, making merry without them, Kick them down Stairs, and force them to rub off.

Smock-fac'd, fair Snout.

Smoke, to Smoke or Smell a Design. *It is Smok't*, it is made Public, all have notice. *Smoke him, Smoke him again*, to affront a Stranger at his coming in.

Smoker, a Vessel to Blind the Enemies, to make way for the *Machine* to Play; also a Tobacconist.

Smoky, c. Jealous. *No Smoke but there is some Fire as no Reeds but there is some Water*, of a thing that will out, because Smoke is a sign of one, and Reeds or Rushes of the other.

Smug, a Black-smith; also neat and spruce.

Smuglers, c. those that Cheat the King of his Customs by private Imports and Exports.

Smutty, Bawdy.

Snack, c. share or part, *to go Snacks*, c. to go halves or share and share alike. *Tip me my Snack, or else I'll Whiddle*, c. Give me my share, or I'll tell.

Snaffle, c. a Highway-man that has got Booty.

Snaggs, large Teeth, also Snails.

Snappish, (a Man) peevish, quarrelsom; (a Dog) apt to Bite.

Snapt, Taken, Caught.

Sneak, c. *goes upon the Sneak at Munns*, c. he privately gets into Houses or Shops at Night, and Steals undiscover'd. *A Sneaking Budge*, c. one that Robbs alone.

Sneaker, (of Punch) a small Bowl.

Sneaking, sheepish, or mean-spirited.

Snearing, flickering, fleering.

Snickering, Laughing in his Sleeve or privately.

Snilch, c. to Eye or See any Body. *The Cull Snilches*, c. the man Eyes you or Sees you.

Snitch, c. *Snitchel*, c. a Filip on the Nose.

Snite, c. to Wipe, or Flap. *Snite his Snitch*, c. Wipe his Nose, or give him a good Flap on the Face. *Sniting*, a Hawk's Sneezing.

Sniveling-Fellow, a Whining Fellow.

Snow-broth, Snow-water.

Snub, to Check, or Rebuke.

Snuff, Pet; also Tobacco taken in Snush.

Snuffle, to Speak through the Nose from a Cold or worse.

Snudge, c. one that lurks under a bed, to watch an opportunity to Rob the House.

Sock, c. a Pocket; also to Beat. *Not a Rag in my Sock*, c. I han't a Farthing in my Pocket. *I'll Sock ye*, c. I'll Drub ye tightly.

Socket-money, Demanded and Spent upon Marriage.

Soft, Foolish.

Sohoe, Seehoe, said aloud at the starting a Hare.

Soker, a Toper, or Fuddle-cap. *An old Soker*, a true Pitcher-man. *To set Soking*, to ply the Pot.

Soldier's-bottle, a large one.

Solomon, c. the Mass.

Son of {
    Apollo, a Scholar.
    Mars, Soldier.
    Venus, a Lover of Women.
    Mercury, a Wit.
    Parclement, a Lawyer.
}

Sooterkin, a By-word upon the Dutch Women, from a Maggot, or Fancy, that their using Stoves so much, Breeds a kind of Animal in their Wombs, like a Mouse, which at their Delivery skips out.

Soreth, the Footings of a Hare in the open Field.

Sorrel-pate, red Hair'd.

Sorter, (at the Post Office) that puts or Digests the Letters into Order or Method.

Soul-driver, a Parson. *He is a Soul*, or loves Brandy. *Of a Noble Soul*, very generous. *A Narrow-Soul'd Fellow*, a poor-spirited, or stingy Fellow.

Souldiers Mawn'd, c. a Counterfeit Sore or Wound in the Left Arm.

Sounder, a Company of Swine, or wild-Boars.

Soupe, Broth, Porridge.

Souse. Not a Souse, not a Penny. (French Money).

Sow's-baby, a Pig.

Sowse-crown, a Fool.

Sow-child, a Female Child. *He has the wrong Sow by the Ear*, or is in a wrong Box.

Sowre, Crabb'd, Surly, Ill-conditioned.

Soyl, when any Deer is hard Hunted, and betakes himself to Swimming in any River.

Spangles, c. ends of Gold or Silver.

Spanish-gout, the Pox.

Spanish-money, fair Words and Compliments.

Spark, a spruce, trim, gay Fellow. *A lewd Spark*, a Man of the Town, or Debaucheé.

Sparring-blows, the first Strokes to try the goodness of young Cocks Heels; also those in a Battel before the Cocks come to Mouth it.

Sparrow-mouth'd, a Mouth o Heavenly wide, as Sir *P. Sidney* calls it.

Speckt-wiper, c. a colour'd Handkerchief.

Spider-catcher, a Spindle for a Man.

Spider's-web, the subtilties of Logic, which (as *Aristo* the Chiote said) tho' artificial to sight, were yet of no Use.

Spill, a small Reward or gift of Money.

Spindle-shankt, very small-legg'd.

Spirit-away, as *Kidnap*.

Spiritual-flesh-broker, a Parson.

Spitter, a red Male Hart of a Year old.

Splenetic, Melancholic.

Split-fig, a Grocer.

Splitter-of-Causes, a Lawyer.

Split my windpipe, a foolish kind of a Curse among the *Beaux*.

Spraints, the Excrements of an Otter.

Spring a Partridge, c. People drawn in, to be *Bit*. *To Spring Partridge's*, to raise them. *A Springe*, a Snare, or Nooze to catch Hares, as a Ginn is a Snare or Nooze to catch Birds.

Spunge, to drink at others Cost. *Spunging-house*, a By-prison. *A Spunging Fellow*, one that lives upon the rest and Pays nothing.

Squab, a very fat, truss Person, a new Hatcht Chick; also a Couch.

Squinte-fuego, one that Squints very much.

Squeek, c. to discover, or impeach; also to cry out. *They Squeek beef upon us*, c. cry out High-way-men or Thieves after us. *The Cull Squeek's*, c. the Rogue Peaches.

Squeeker, c. a Barboy; also a Bastard, or any other child.
  Stifle the Squeeker, c. to Murder the Child and throw it
  into a House of Office.
Squawl, to throw a wry; also to cry a loud.
Squeemish, nice.
Squeeze, to gripe, or skrew hard.
Squeezing of Wax, being Bound for any Body; also sealing of
  Writings.
Squire of Alsatia, a Man of Fortune, drawn in, cheated, and
  ruin'd by a pack of poor lowsy, spunging, bold Fellows
  that liv'd (formerly) in White-Fryers. *The Squire*, a Sir
  Timothy Treat-all; also a Sap-pate. *Squirish*, foolish; also
  one that pretends to Pay all Reckonings, and is not
  strong enough in the Pocket. *A fat Squire*, a rich Fool.
Stag, *Staggard*, see *Hart*.
Stallion, c. a Whore-Master; also a Stone-Horse kept to
  cover Mares.
Stall-whimper, c. a Bastard.
Stalling, c. making or ordaining.
Stalling-ken, c. a Broker's Shop, or any House that receives
  stolen Goods.
Stale { *Jest*, old, dull.
         { *Maid*, at her last Prayers.
Stam-flesh, c. to Cant.
Stammel, a brawny, lusty, strapping Wench.
Stamps, c. Legs.
Stampers, c. Shoes; also Carriers.
Starched, affected, proud, stiff.
Start, (Drink) Brewers emptying several Barrels into a
  great Tub, and thence conveying it through a Leather-
  pipe down the Cellar into the Butts.

Starter, c. a Question. *I am no Starter*, I shan't flinch, or cry to go Home.

Start the Hare, put her up.

Statues, either Images in Brass or Stone, or Men without motion.

Steenkirk, a Muslin-neckcloath carelesly put on, first, at the Battel of *Steenkirk*, afterwards a Fashion for both Sexes.

Steppony, a Decoction of Raisins of the Sun, and Lemons in Conduit-water, sweetned with Sugar and Bottled up.

Stern, the Tail of a Wolf; also the hind part of a Ship.

Stick-flamms, c. a pair of Gloves.

Stickle-bag, a very small prickly Fish, without Scales, a choice Bait for a Trout. *A great Stickler*, a zealous Man in the Cause or Interest he espouses. *It Sticks in his Stomack*, he resents it.

Stiff, Stiff-rump, proud, stately.

Sting-bum, a Niggard.

Stingo, humming, strong Liquor.

Stingy, covetous, close-fisted, sneaking.

Stitch, a Tayler.

Stitch-back, very strong Ale.

Stock-jobbing, a sharp, cunning, cheating Trade of Buying and Selling. Shares of Stock in East-India, Guinea and other Companies; also in the Bank, Exchequer, &c.

Stock-drawers, Stockings.

Stone { *Dead*, quite.
{ *Doublet*, a Prison.

Stop-hole Abbey, c. the Nick-name of the chief Rendezvouz of the Canting Crew of *Gypsies, Beggers, Cheats, Thieves, &c.*

Stop my Vitals, a silly Curse in use among the *Beaux*.

Stoter, c. a great Blow. *Stoter him*, c. or *tip him a Stoter*, c. settle him, give him a swinging Blow.

Stout, very strong, Malt-Drink.

Stow, c. you have said enough. *Stow you bene Cove*, c. hold your Peace good Fellow. *Stow your Whidds and Plant 'em; for the Cove of the Ken can cant 'em*, Take care what you say, for the Man of the House understands you; also to hoard Treasure, or lay up Corn in Granaries or Drink in Cellars. Hence Stoward, or Steward.

Strain-hard, to ly heartily.

Strait-lac'd, precise, squeemish, puritanical, nice.

Straping, c. lying with a Wench.

Strapping-Lass, a swinging two-handed Woman.

Stress of weather, foul weather at Sea. *At a Stress*, at a pinch.

Stretching, hanging. *He'll Stretch for it*, he'll be Hang'd. *He Stretcht hard*, told a whisking Ly.

Stretcher, the piece of Wood that lies cross the Boat, where on the Water-man rests his Feet.

Strike, c. to Beg, to Rob; also to borrow Money. *Strike all the Cheats*, c. Rob all you meet. *Strike the Cull*, c. Beg of that Gentleman. *Strike the Cly*, c. get that Fellow's Money from him. *He has Struck the Quidds*, c. he has got the *Cole* from him. *He Strikes every Body*, c. he borrows Money every where, he runs in every one's Debt. *A Strike*, (of Corn) a Bushel.

Strip, c. to Rob or *Gut* a House, to unrig any Body, or to *Bite* them of their Money. *Strip the Ken*, c. to *Gut* the House. *Strip the Table*, c. to Winn all the Money on the Place. *Stripts*, poor, Naked. *We have Stript the Cull*, c. We have got all the Fool's Money. *The Cove's Stript*, c. the Rogue has not a *Jack* left to help himself.

Strommel, c. Straw.

Strowlers, c. Vagabonds, Itinerants, Men of no settled Abode, of a Precarious Life. Wanderers of Fortune, such, as, Gypsies, Beggers, Pedlers, Hawkers, Mountebanks, Fidlers, Country-Players, Rope-dancers, Juglers, Tumblers, showers of Tricks, and Raree-show-men.

Strowling-morts, c. pretending to be Widows, sometimes Travel the Countries, making Laces upon Ewes, Beggers-tape, *&c.* Are light Finger'd, Subtil, Hypocritical, Cruel, and often dangerous to meet, especially when a *Ruffler* is with them.

Study, a Closet of Books. *In a brown Study*, musing, pensive, careful.

Strum, c. a Periwig. *Rum-strum*, c. a long Wig; also a handsom Wench, or Strumpet.

Stuff, Nonsense, idle, ridiculous, impertinent Talk.

Stuling-ken, c. as *Stalling-ken*, c.

Stum, the Flower of fermenting Wine, used by Vintners, when their Wine is down or flat, to make it Drink up and brisk; also when they Brew, to make their mixtures, (by putting them into a new Ferment) all of one Taste. *Stumm'd Wines are very unwholesom, and may be discover'd, by a white Froth round the sides of the Glass.*

Stubble-it, c. hold your Tongue.

Sturdy-beggers, c. the fifth and last of the most ancient Order of Canters.

Sub-beau, or *Demibeau*, a wou'd-be-fine.

Sub-bois, Maples, Birch, Sallow, and Willow.

Suck, c. Wine or strong Drink. *This is rum Suck*, c. it is excellent Tipple. *We'll go and Suck our Faces, but if they*

toute us, we'll take rattle and brush, c. let's go to Drink
and be merry, but if we be Smelt, by the People of the
House, we must Scower off. *He loves to Suck his Face*, he
delights in Drinking.

Suckey, c. drunkish, maudlin, half Seas o'er.

Suit and Cloak, good store of Brandy or any agreable Liquor,
let down Gutter-lane.

Sun-burnt, having many (Male) Children.

Sunny-bank, a good, rousing Winter-Fire.

Superstitious-Pies, Minc'd, or Christmas-Pies, so Nick-nam'd
by the *Puritans*, or *Precisians*, tho' they can Eat 'em; but
affecting to be singular, make them a Month or six
Weeks before Christmas, or the Feast of Christ.

Supernaculum, not so much as a Drop left to be poured
upon the Thumb-nail, so cleaverly was the Liquor
tipt off.

Supouch, c. an Hostess or Landlady.

Surtout, a loose, great, or riding Coat.

Sutler, c. he that Pockets up, Gloves, Knives,
Handkerchiefs, Snuff and Tobacco-boxes, and all the
lesser Moveables; also a Scullion or Huckster, one that
follows an Army, to sell Meat, Drink, *&c.*

Swadlers, c. the tenth Order of the Canting Tribe. *To
Swaddle*, to Beat lustily with, a Cane or Cable's end. *I'll
Swaddle your Hide*, I'll bang your Back.

Swag, c. a Shop. *Rum Swag*, c. full of rich Goods.

Swagger, to vapour or bounce.

Swallow, (Falsities for Truths) to believe them.

Sweets, the Dreggs of Sugar used by Vintners, to allay the
undue fermenting or fretting of their Wine.

Sweetners, c. Guinea-Droppers, Cheats, Sharpers. *To Sweeten*,

c. to decoy, draw in, and *Bite*. *To be Sweet upon*, c. to coakse, wheedle, entice or allure.

Swig-men, c. the 13*th* Rank of the Canting Crew, carrying small Habberdashery-Wares about, pretending to sell them, to colour their Roguery, *A hearty Swig*, a lusty Draught. *To Swig it off*, to Drink it all up.

Swill-belly, a great Drinker.

Swimmer, a Counterfeit (old) Coyn.

Swinging $\begin{cases} Clap, \\ Lye, \\ Fellow, \end{cases}$ a very great one.

I *Swing'd him off*, I lay'd on and beat him well-favoredly. He is *Swing'd off*, damnably Clapt.

Swinish, (fellow) raking, greedy, gluttonous, covetous.

Swabbers, the Ace of Hearts, Knave of Clubs, Ace and Duce of Trumps; also the Sorriest Sea-Men put to Wash and clean the Ship.

Swop, to barter or Truck.

T

Tackle, a Mistress; also good Cloths. *The Cull has tipt his Tackle Rum-rigging*, c. or, *has Tipt his Bloss Rum-tackle*, c. the keeping Coxcomb has given his Mistress very fine Cloths.

Taffy, a Welshman or David. *Taffy's Day*, the first of March.

Tables, a Game. *Turn the Tables*, make it your own Case.

Take the Culls in, c. Seize the Men, in order to Rob them.

Take-time, never to thrust but with advantage. *Very taking*, acceptable, agreeable, or becoming. *It Takes well* or, *the Town Takes it*, the Play pleas'd, or was acted with Applause, or the Book Sells well. *No doubt but it will Take*, no question but it will sell.

Talent, the same with Capacity, Genius, Inclination or Ability; also 375 *l.* in Silver, and 4500 *l.* in Gold. *His Talent does not lye that way*, he has no Genius for it, or his Head does not lean to it.

Tale-tellers, a sort of Servants in use with the great Men in *Ireland*, to Lull them a sleep with Tales and Stories of a Cock and a Bull, *&c. I tell you my Tale, and my Tales-man*, or Author.

Tall-boy, a Pottle or two Quart-pot full of Wine.

Talons, or *Pounces*, a Bird's Claws as Fangs are Beast's Claws.

Tally-men, Brokers that let out Cloths at moderate Rates to wear per Week, Month, or Year.

Tame-fellow, tractable, easy, manageable.

Tamper, to practise upon one.

Tant, *Tantest*, Mast of a Ship or Man, Tall, Tallest.

Tantivy-boies, high-Flyers, or High-flown Church-men, in opposition, to the moderate Church-men; or Latitudinarians a lower sort of Flyers, like Batts, between Church-men and Dissenters.

Taplash, Wretched, sorry Drink, or Hog-wash.

Tappeth, see, *Beateth*.

Tariff, a Book of Rates or Customs; also another of the Current Coin.

Tarnish, to Fade.

Tar, *Tarpaulin*, a Sea-man; also a piece of Canvas (tarr'd) laid over the Hatches to keep out Wet.

Tar-terms, proper Sea-Phrases, or Words.

Tart-dame, sharp, quick.

Tartar, a sharper. *To catch a Tartar*, in stead of catching, to be catcht in a Trap.

Tatter-de-mallion, c. a ragged, tatter'd Begger sometimes half Naked, with design to move Charity, having better Cloths at Home. *In Tatters*, in Raggs. *Tatter'd and Torn*, rent and torn.

Tattler, c. an Alarm, or Striking Watch, or (indeed) any.

Tatts, c. false Dice.

Tat-monger, c. a Sharper, or Cheat, using false Dice.

Tatling { *Fellow*, or / *Woman*, } prating, impertinent.

Taunts, Girds, Quips, or Jeers. *To Taunt*, to Jeer or Flout.

Taudry, garish, gawdy, with Lace or mismatched and staring Colours: A Term borrow'd from those times when they Trickt and Bedeckt the Shrines and Altars of the Saints, as being at vye with each other upon that occasion. The Votaries of St. *Audrey* (an Isle of *Ely* Saint) exceeding all the rest in the Dress and Equipage of her Altar, it grew into a Nay-word, upon any thing very Gawdy, that it was all Taudry, as much as to say all St. *Audrey*.

Tayle, c. a Sword. *Tayle-drawers*, c. Sword-stealers. *He drew the Cull's Tayle rumly*, c. he whipt away the Gentleman's Sword cleverly.

Teague-land, Ireland.

Teague-landers, Irish-men.

Tears of the Tankard, drops of the good Liquor that fall beside.

Tegg, see *Doe*.

Temperade, an East-Indian-dish, now in use in *England*, being a Fowl Fricasied, with high Sauce, Blancht Almonds and Rice.

Temperament, an Expedient or Medium; also a due proportion of the four Humors.

Temple-pickling, the Pumping of Bailives, Bumms, Setters, Pick-pockets, *&c.*

Tender-parnel, a very nicely Educated creature, apt to catch Cold upon the least blast of Wind.

Terce, the Nails of the Sword-hand quite down.

Tercel-gentle, a Knight or Gentleman of a good Estate; also any rich Man.

Terra-firma, an Estate in Land; also a Continent.

Has the Cull any Terra Firma? Has the Fool any Land?

That That or *There*, to a Hare.

Thwack, to Beat with a Stick or Cudgel.

The Dragon upon St. George, c. the Woman uppermost.

Thief-takers, who make a Trade of helping People (for a gratuity) to their lost Goods and sometimes for Interest or Envy snaping the Rogues themselves; being usually in fee with them, and acquainted with their Haunts.

Thorn-back, an old Maid; also a well known Fish, said to be exceeding Provocative.

Thorough-cough, farting at the same time.

Thorough-passage, in at one Ear, and out at t'other.

Thorough-stitch, over Shoes, over Boots.

The Three-Legged-stool, Tyburn.

Three-threads, half common Ale, and the rest Stout or Double Beer.

Threpps, c. Three-pence.

Thrumms, c. Three-pence. *Tip me Thrumms*, c. Lend me Three-pence.

Thummikins, a Punishment (in *Scotland*) by hard Squeezing or Pressing of the Thumbs to extort Confession, which Stretches them prodigiously and is very painful. In Camps, and on board of Ships, lighted Matches are clapt between the Fingers to the same intent.

Tib, a young Lass.

Tib of the Buttery, c. a Goose.

Tickrum, c. a Licence. *to run a tick*, to go on the Score, or a trust.

Tickle-pitcher, a Toss-pot, or Pot-companion.

Tiffing, c. lying with a Wench.

Tilter, a Sword, *to tilt*, to fight with Rapier, or pushing

Swords, *run a tilt*, a swift Pursuit, also Drink made to
run faster.

Tint for tant, hit for hit, and dash for dash.

Tip, c. to give or lend; also Drink and a draught. *Tip your
Lour*, or *Cole or I'll Mill ye*, c. give me your Money or
I'll kill ye. *Tip the Culls a Sock, for they are sawcy*, c.
Knock down the Men for resisting. *Tip the Cole to Adam
Tiler*, c. give your Pick-pocket Money presently to your
running Comrade. *Tip the Mish*, c. give me the Shirt.
Tip me a Hog, c. lend me a Shilling. *Tip it all off*, Drink it
all off at a Draught. *Don't spoil his Tip*, don't baulk his
Draught. *A Tub of good Tip*, (for Tipple) a Cask of
strong Drink. *To Tip off*, to Dye.

Tipler, a Fuddle-cap or Toss-pot.

Tipsy, a'most Drunk.

Tiring, Dressing; also when a Leg or Pinion of a Pullet,
Pigeon, *&c.* is given to a Hawk to pluck at. *Tiring-room*,
a Dressing-Room. *A Tire-woman*, one that teaches to
Dress in the Hair, when in Fashion, and when out, to
cut the Hair, and Dress the Head.

Tit-bit, a fine Snack, or choice Morsel.

Tit-tat, the aiming of Children to go at first.

Tittle-tattle, foolish, idle, impertinent Talk.

Titter, to Laugh at a Feather.

Titter-totter, who is upon the Reel, at every jog, or Blast of
Wind.

Toge, c. a Coat.

Togemans, c. a Gown or Cloak. *I have Bit the Togemans*, c. I
have Stole the Cloak. *'Tis a Rum-togemans*, 'tis a good
Camlet-Cloak, *Let's nim it*, c. let's whip it off.

Tokens, the Plague, also Presents from one to another, and

Farthings. *Not a Token left*, not one Farthing remaining. *Tom-fool's-token*, Money.

Tol. Toledo, c. a Sword. *Bite the Tol*, c. to Steal the Sword. *A Rum-tol*, c. a Silver-hilted Sword. *A Queer-tol*, c. a Brass or Steel-hilted or ord'nary Sword.

Tom-boy, a Ramp, or *Tomrig*.

Tom of Bedlam, c. the same as *Abram-man*.

Tom-conney, a very silly Fellow.

Tom rig, a Ramp.

Tom-thumb, a Dwarf or diminitive Fellow. *Come by Tom Long the Carrier*, of what is very late, or long a coming.

Tongue-pad, a smooth, Glib-tongued, insinuating Fellow.

Tony, a silly Fellow, or Ninny. *A meer Tony*, or Simpleton.

Tool, an Implement fit for any Turn, the Creature of any Cause or Faction; a meer Property, or Cat's Foot.

Top, c. to Cheat, or Trick any one; also to Insult. *What do you Top upon me?* c. do you stick a little Wax to the Dice to keep them together, to get the Chance, you wou'd have? *He thought to have to Topt upon me*, c. he design'd to have Put upon me, Sharpt me, Bullied me, or Affronted me.

Tope, to Drink. *An old Toper*, a staunch Drunkard. *To Tope it about*, or *Dust it about*, to Drink briskly about.

Top-diver, a Lover of Women. *An old Top-diver*, one that has Lov'd *Old-hat* in his time.

Top-heavy, Drunk.

Topping-fellow, who has reacht the Pitch and greatest Eminence in any Art; the Master, and the Cock of his Profession.

Topping-cheat, c. the Gallows.

Topping-cove, c. the Hangman.

Torch-cul, the same as *Bum-fodder*.

Torcoth, a Fish having a red Belly, found only in the Pool *Sinperis*, in *Carnarvanshire*.

Tories, Zealous Sticklers for the Prerogative and Rights of the Crown, in behalf of the Monarchy; also Irish-thieves, or *Rapparies*.

Tost, to name or begin a new Health. *Who Tosts now?* Who Christens the Health? *A old Tost*, a pert pleasant old Fellow.

Totty-headed, Giddy-headed, Hare-brain'd.

Tout, c. to look out Sharp, to be upon one's Guard. *Who Touts?* c. who looks out sharp? *Tout the Culls*, c. Eye those Folks which way they take. *Do you Bulk and I'll File*, c. if you'll jostle him, I will Pick his Pocket.

Touting-ken, c. a Tavern or Ale-house Bar.

Tourn, Copulation of Roes.

Tower-hill-play, a slap on the Face and a kick on the Breech.

Town-bull, one that rides all the Women he meets.

Tower, a Woman's false Hair on their Foreheads. *Towring Thoughts*, Ambitious Aspiring. *To Tower*, to sore on High. *They have been round the Tower with it*, c. that piece of Money has been Clipt.

Trace, the Footing of a Hare in the Snow.

Track, c. to go.

Track up the Dancers, c. whip up the Stairs.

Tract, the footing of a Boar.

Train, a Hawk's or Peacock's Tail; also Attendants or Retinue.

Trajoning, when a Roe crosses and doubles.

Tansnear, c. to come up with any body.

Translators, Sellers of old Shoes and Boots, between Shoe-makers and Coblers; also that turn or Translate one Language into another.

Transmogrify, to alter, or new vamp.

Tranter, the same as *Crocker*.

Trapan, c. he that draws in or wheedles a *Cull*, and *Bites* him. *Trapan'd*, c. Sharpt, ensnar'd.

Trapes, a dangling Slattern.

Trassing, when the Hawk raiseth any Fowl aloft, and soaring with it, at length descendeth with it to the Ground.

Tree the Martern, Dislodge him.

Treewins, c. Three-pence.

Trigry-mate, an idle She-Companion.

Trib, c. a Prison. *He is in Trib*, for *Tribulation*, c. he is layd by the Heels, or in a great deal of Trouble.

Trim, Dress. in *a sad Trim*, Dirty, Undrest. *A Trim-Lad*, a spruce, neat, well trickt Man.

Trimmer, a moderate, betwixt *Whig* and *Tory*, between Prerogative and Property. *To Trim*, to hold fair with both sides. *Trim the Boat*, poise it. *Trim of the Ship*, that way she goes best.

Trimming, c. Cheating People of their Money.

Trine, c. to Hang; also Tyburn. *Trining*, c. Hanging.

Trinkets, Porringers, and also any little odd thing, Toies and Trifles.

Tringum-Trangum, a Whim, or Maggot.

Tripolin, Chalk, nicknam'd and us'd by the *French* Perfumers as *Alabaster* is by the *English*.

Trip, a short Voyage or Journey; also an Error of the Tongue, or Pen, a stumble, a false step, a miscarriage, or a Bastard.

Troateth, see *Growneth*.

Trotters, Feet, usually Sheeps. *Shake your Trotters*, troop off, be gone. *An old Trot*, a sorry base old Woman. *A Dog Trot*, a pretty Pace.

Troll-away, bowl away, or trundle away.

Troll-about, saunter, loiter, wander about.

Trolly-lolly, coarse Lace once much in fashion, now worn only by the meaner sort.

Trollop. A great Trollop, a lusty coarse Ramp or Tomrig.

Trooper, c. a half Crown.

Trounc'd, troubled, Cast in Law, Punisht. *I'll Trounce the Rogue*, I'll hamper him.

Truck, to swop or barter.

Trug, a dirty Puzzel, an ord'nary sorry Woman; also the third part of a Bushel, and a Tray for Milk.

Trull, c. a Whore; also a Tinker's travelling Wife or Wench, and to trundle.

Trumpery, old Ware, old Stuff, as old Hatts, Boots, Shoes, &c. Trash and Trumpery. *For want of good Company, welcome Trumpery.*

Trundlers, c. Pease.

Trunk, c. a Nose; also the body of a Tree, or Man, without Head, Arms or Leggs. *How fares your old Trunk?* c. Does your Nose stand fast?

Trusty-Trojan, or *Trusty-Trout*, a sure Friend or Confident.

Tuck't, Hang'd.

Tumbler, c. a Cart. *To shove the Tumbler*, c. to be Whipt at the Cart's Tail; also one that Decoys, or draws others into Play, and one that shows Tricks with and without a Hoop; a low Silver Cup to Drink out of, and a Coney Dog.

Tup, Copulation of Ram and Ewe. *Venison out of Tup-park*, Mutton.

Turk, any cruel hard-hearted Man.

Turky-Merchants, drivers of Turkies.

Turkish-shore, Lambeth, Southwark and Roderhith-side of the Water.

Turkish Treatment, very sharp or ill dealing in Business.

Turn-coat, he that quits one and embraces another Party.

Turnep-pate, White or Fair-hair'd.

Twang, a smack or ill Taste.

Tweak, *in a Tweak*, in a heavy taking, much-vext, or very angry.

Twelver, c. a Shilling.

Twist, half Tea, half Coffee; also a Bough, and to Eat. *To Twist lustily*, to Feed like a Farmer.

Twit, to hit in the Teeth.

Twitter, to Laugh much with little Noise; also to Tremble.

U V

Vagaries, wild Rambles, extravagant Frolicks.

Vagrant, a wandring Rogue, a strolling Vagabond.

Vain, Fond.

Vain-glorious, or *Ostentatious Man*, one that Pisses more than he Drinks.

Valet, a Servant.

Vamp, c. to Pawn any thing; also a Sock. *I'll Vamp and tip you the Cole*, c. I'll Pawn my Cloths, but I'll raise the Money for you. *To Vamp*, to new Dress, Licker, Refresh, or Rub up old Hatts Boots, Shoes, *&c.*

Vampers, c. Stockings.

Varlets, Rogues, Rascals, *&c.* now tho' formerly Yeomans Servants.

Vaudois, Inhabitants of the Vallies in *Piedmont*, Subject to the Duke of *Savoy*, fam'd for their frequent Rencounters with and Defeating of French Parties, intercepting their Provisions, *&c.*

Vault, an arched Cellar, and House of Office. *She goes to the Vault*, when a Hare (which is very seldom) takes the Ground like a Coney.

Vaulting-School, c. a Bawdy-house; also an Academy where Vaulting, and other Manly Exercises are Taught.

Vauntlay, Hounds or Beagles set in readiness, expecting the Chace to come by, and then cast off before the rest come in.

Velvet, c. a Tongue. *Tip the Velvet*, c. to Tongue a Woman.

Venary, or *Venery*, Hunting or Chasing Beasts and Birds of Venery, as, the Hart, the Hind, the Hare, Boar and Wolf, the Pheasant, the Partridge, *&c.*

Venison, whatsoever Beast of the Forest is for the food of Man.

Vent, the fundament of Poultry and Fish; also a Bung-hole in a Vessel.

Vent the Otter, see *Otter*.

Vessels, several Pipes and Conveyances in the body, of the Blood, Seed, Serum or Urine, as the Bloud-vessels, Lymphæ-ducts, Spermatick Vessels, Urinary Vessels, *&c.* Also Kitchin-Utensils, as Pots, Pans, *&c.* And of other Offices, as Brewing, Washing Churning Vessels, *&c.*

View, the Treading of a Buck or Fallow Deer.

Vinegar, c. a Cloak.

Virago, a masculine Woman, or a great two-handed Female.

Virtuoso, an experimental Philosopher, a Trader in new Inventions and Discoveries, a Projecter in Philosophy.

Unharbour the Hart, see *Hart*.

Unitarians, a numerous Sect holding one God without plurality or distinction of Persons.

Unkennel the Fox, Dislodge him.

Unrig'd, Stript, Undrest, and Ships that are laid up. *Unrig the Drab*, c. to pull all the Whore's Cloths off.

Untwisted, Undone, Ruin'd.

Unwasht-bawdry, Rant, errant fulsom Bawdry.

Uphils, high Dice.

Vouchers, c. that put off False Money for Sham-coyners; also one that Warrants Gagers or under Officers Accompts, either at the Excize-Office, or else where.

Uppish, rampant, crowing, full of Money. *He is very Uppish*, well lined in the Fob; also brisk.

Upright-men, c. the second Rank of the Canting Tribes, having sole right to the first night's Lodging with the *Dells*. *Go Upright*, said by Taylers and Shoe-makers, to their Servants, when any Money is given to make them Drink and signifies, bring it all out in Drink, tho' the Donor intended less and expects Change or some return of Money.

Upstarts, new rais'd to Honour.

Urchin, a little sorry Fellow; also a Hedge-hog.

Urines, Netts to catch Hawks.

Urinal of the Planets, Ireland, with us, because of its frequent and great Rains, as *Heidelberg*, and *Cologn* in *Germany*, have the same Name upon the same Account; also a Chamber-pot, or Glass.

Utopia, Fairy-Land, a new Atlantis, or Isle of Pines.

W

Waddle, to go like a Duck.

Wag, Waggish, Arch, Gamesom, Pleasant.

Wag-Tail, a light Woman.

Wallowish, a malkish, ill Taste.

Wap, c. to Lie with a Man. *If she won't wap for a Winne, let her trine for a Make*, c. If she won't Lie with a Man for a Penny, let her Hang for a Half-penny. *Mort wap-apace* c. a Woman of Experience, or very expert at the Sport.

Wapper-eyed, that has Sore or running Eyes.

Warm, well lined or flush in the Pocket.

Warming-pan, an old fashion'd large Watch. *A Scotch Warming-pan*, a She-bed-fellow.

Warren, c. he that is Security for Goods taken up, on Credit, by Extravagant young Gentlemen; also a Boarding-school and a Bawdy-house.

Wash, After-wort; also Paint for Faces.

Waspish, peevish.

Water-Pad, c. one that Robbs Ships in the Thames.

Wattles, Ears; also Sheep-folds.

Weak, Silly, half-witted.

Welsh-Camp, a Field betwixt Lambs-Conduit and Grays
  Inn-lane, where the Mob got to gether in great
  numbers, doing great mischief.

Welsh-fiddle, the Itch.

Westminster-Wedding, a Whore and a Rogue Married
  together.

Wet-Quaker, a Drunkard of that Sect.

Wheadle, c. a Sharper. *To cut a Wheadle*, c. to Decoy, by
  Fawning and Insinuation.

Wheel-band in the Nick, regular Drinking over the left
  Thumb.

*When we enter'd the Ken, we loapt up the Dancers, and Fagotted
  all there*, c. when we got into the House, we whipt up
  Stairs and Bound all the People there.

Wheatgear, a Bird smaller than a Dottrel, choice *Peck*.

Whether-go-ye, a Wife.

Whet, a Draught or Sup to encourage the Appetite.

Whet-stones-park, a Lane betwixt Holborn and Lincolns-Inn-
  fields, fam'd for a Nest of Wenches now de-park'd.

Whids, c. Words.

Whiddle, c. to tell, or discover. *He Whiddles*, c. he Peaches.
  He Whiddles the whole Scrap, c. he discovers all he knows.
  The Cull has Whiddled, because we wou'd n't tip him a Snack,
  c. the Dog has discover'd, because we did n't give him a
  share. *They Whiddle beef, and we must Brush*, c. they cry
  out Thieves, we are Pursued, and must Fly.

Whiddler, c. a Peacher (or rather Impeacher) of his Gang.

Whiggs, the Republicans or Common-wealths-men, under
  the Name of Patriots, and Lovers of Property; originally
  the Field-conventiclers in the West of *Scotland*.

Whiggish, Factious, Seditious, Restless, Uneasy.

Whig-land, Scotland.

Whip-shire, Yorkshire.

Whipster, a sharp, or subtil Fellow.

Whip off, c. to Steal, to Drink cleaverly, to Snatch, and to run away. *Whipt through the Lungs*, run through the Body with a Sword. *Whip in at the Glaze*, c. got in at the Window.

Whim, a Maggot.

Whimsical, Maggotish.

Whimper, a low, or small Cry. *What a Whimpering you keep?*

Whindle, a low or feigned Crying.

Whineth, see *Otter*. *To Whine*, to cry squeekingly, as at Conventicles.

Whinyard, a Sword.

Whipper-snapper, a very small but sprightly Boy.

Whip-Jacks, c. the tenth Order of the Canting Crew; Counterfeit Mariners Begging with false Passes, pretending Shipwrecks, great Losses at Sea, &c. narrow escapes; telling dismal Stories, having learnt *Tar-terms* on purpose, but are meer Cheats.

Whirlegigs, Testicles.

Whisk, a little inconsiderable, impertinent Fellow.

Whisker, a great Lie.

Whiskins, c. shallow, brown Bowls to Drink out off.

Whistle, a derisory Term for the Throat. *Wet your Whistle*, to Liquor your Throat.

Whit, c. Newgate. *As five Rum-padders, are Rub'd in the Darkman's out of the Whit, and are pik'd in to the Deuseaville*, c. five Highway-men in the Night broke Newgate and are gone into the Countrey.

White-liver'd, Cowardly; also Pale Visag'd.

White-wool, c. Silver.

White-chappel-portion, two torn Smocks, and what Nature gave.

Whow-ball, a Milk-maid.

Whur, the rising or fluttering of Partridge or Pheasant.

Wicket, c. a Casement, also a little Door. *As toute through the Wicket, and see where a Cully pikes with his Gentry-mort, whose Munns are the Rummest I ever touted before*, c. look through the Casement and see where the Man walks with a Gentle-woman, whose Face is the fairest, I have ever seen.

Wicher-Cully, c. a Silver-smith.

Wide, when the Biass of the Bowl holds not enough.

Widows-Weeds, Mourning Cloths. *A Grass-Widow*, one that pretends to have been Married, but never was, yet has Children.

Whores-kitling, a Bastard.

Whore-son, a Bastard.

Wild-boar, the fourth Year, at which Age or a little before he leaveth the *Sounder*, and is called a *Singler*, or *Sanglier*, *Hogsteer*, the third Year; *Hog*, the second Year; *Pig of the Sounder*, the first Year. *A Boar coucheth*, Lodgeth; *Rear the Boar*, Dislodge him. *A Boar freemeth*, maketh a noise at rutting Time.

Wild-Rogues, c. the fifth Order of Canters, such as are train'd up from Children to *Nim* Buttons off Coats, to creep in at Cellar and Shop-Windows, and to slip in at Doors behind People; also that have been whipt, Burnt in the Fist and often in Prison for Roguery.

Wiles, Engins to take Deer; also Tricks Intrigues.

Wily, cunning crafty, intriguing.

Willing-Tit, a little Horse that Travels chearfully.

Willow, c. Poor, and of no Reputation.

Wind-fall, a great Fortune fallen unexpectedly by the Death of a Friend, or Wood fell by high Winds, *&c.*

Wind-mills in the Head, empty Projects. *He'll go as near the Wind as another*, live as thrifty and wary as any one.

Win, c. a Penny. *To Win*, c. to Steal. *Won*, c. Stolen. *The Cull has won a couple of Rum glimsticks*, c. the Rogue has Stole a pair of Silver-Candlesticks.

Windy-fellow, without Sense or Reason.

Wink, c. a Signal or Intimation. *He tipt the Wink*, c. he gave the Sign or Signal.

Wipe, c. a Blow; also a Reflection. *He tipt him a rum Wipe*, c. he gave him a swinging Blow. *I gave him a Wipe*, I spoke something that cut him, or gaul'd him. *He Wipt his Nose*, c. he gull'd him.

Wiper, c. a Handkerchief. *Nim the Wiper*, c. to Steal the Handkerchief.

Wiper-drawer, c. a Handkerchief Stealer. *He drew a broad, narrow, cam, or Speckt Wiper*, c. he Pickt-pockets of a broad, or narrow, Ghenting, Cambrick, or Colour'd Handkerchief.

Wire-draw, c. a Fetch or Trick to wheedle in *Bubbles*; also to screw, over-reach, or deal hard with. *Wire-drawn*, c. so serv'd, or treated.

Wife Man of Gotham, a Fool.

Witcher, c. Silver.

Witcher-bubber, c. a Silver-bowl. *The Cull is pik'd with the Witcher-bubber*, c. the Rogue is marched off with the Silver-Bowl.

Witcher-tilter, c. a Silver-hilted Sword. *He has bit*, or *drawn the Witcher-tilter*, c. he has Stole the Silver-hilted Sword.

Within the Sword, from the Sword to the Right Hand.

Without the Sword, all the Man's-Body above the Sword.

The *Witt*, c. Newgate.

Woman of the Town, a Lewd, common Prostitute.

Womble te-cropt, see *Crop-sick*.

Wooden-ruff, c. a Pillory, the Stocks at the other end. *Hudibras. He wore the Wooden-ruff*, c. he stood in the Pillory.

Wood-pecker, c. a Bystander that bets; also a bird of that Name. *In a Wood*, at a loss.

Wooly-crown, a Fool. *Your Wits are a Wool-gathering, are in a Wild goose-chace.*

Word-pecker, one that play's with Words.

Worm'd out of, Rookt, Cheated, Trickt.

Wreath, the Tail of a Boar; also a Torce between the Mantle and the Crest.

X Y Z

Xantippe, a Scold; also the froward Wife of *Socrates*.

Yarmouth-Capon, a Red Herring.

Yarmouth-Coach, a sorry low Cart to ride on, drawn by one Horse.

Yarmouth-Pie, made of Herrings, highly Spic'd, and Presented by the City of *Norwich*, (upon the forfeiture of their Charter) annually to the King.

Yarum, c. Milk.

Yea and Nay-Men, Quakers.

Yearn, when Beagles bark and cry at their Game.

Yellow, Jealous.

Yellow-boy, c. Piece of Gold of any Coin.

Yeomam of the Mouth, an Officer belonging to his Majestie's Pantry.

Yoak'd, Married.

Yorkshire-Tike, a Yorkshire manner of Man.

Zany, a Mountebank's Merry-Andrew, or Jester, to distinguish him from a Lord's Fool.

Zuche, a wither'd or dry Stock or Stub of a Tree.

FINIS